MISSIONS IN THE WORLD
TODAY
IS VOLUME
100
OF THE

Twentieth Century Encyclopedia of Catholicism
UNDER SECTION
IX
THE CHURCH AND THE MODERN WORLD
IT IS ALSO THE
70TH
VOLUME IN ORDER OF PUBLICATION

Edited by HENRI DANIEL-ROPS of the Académie Française

MISSIONS
IN THE WORLD TODAY

By RENÉ-PIERRE MILLOT

Translated from the French by J. HOLLAND SMITH

HAWTHORN BOOKS · PUBLISHERS · *New York*

First Edition, July, 1961

NIHIL OBSTAT

Daniel Duivesteijn, S.T.D.

Censor Deputatus

IMPRIMATUR

E. Morrogh Bernard

Vicarius Generalis

Westmonasterii, die XV MAII MCMLXI

The Nihil obstat and the Imprimatur are a declaration that a book or pamphlet is considered to be free from doctrinal or moral error. It is not implied that those who have granted the Nihil obstat and Imprimatur agree with the contents, opinions or statements expressed.

CONTENTS

INTRODUCTION

It has become a commonplace to lay stress on the extraordinary progress the world has seen in less than a century and especially since 1900. What has been done, especially in the realms of transport and communications, has rendered worldwide all the problems facing man in the course of the last sixty years, whether in the political or economic fields. When the modern businessman needs no more than a long week-end to go and deal with his business in San Francisco and give an account of it to his board of directors in Paris, how can we remain indifferent to events occurring in Central Africa which in a moment may have repercussions all over the world, from Moscow to the heart of South America, from Paris to Java?

But none of the advances made since the beginning of our century is as spectacular as the fabulous growth of the population of the world during the same period. Between 1900 and 1950, the increase was greater than that between the birth of Christ and 1848—that is, than during a period of eighteen centuries and a half. The population of the world today is 2,600 million—as closely as can be reckoned by statistics—Asia accounting for 50 per cent of them, Europe for 25 per cent, America for 13 per cent, Africa for 8 per cent and Oceania (including Indonesia and the Philippines) for 4 per cent. At the present time the population of the world is growing at a vertiginous rate, by more than one per cent per year. In other words, in every minute that passes the number of the world's inhabitants—allowing for those who die during that same minute—increases by sixty-seven. At this rate, in 1980, there will be in our world 3,500 million people and by 2050, 7,300 million.

Unfortunately, terrible problems arise as a result of this accelerated growth in population: chief among them is over-population, with all its consequences (malnutrition, illiteracy and social distress of all kinds). We might see the world as, so to say, a tragic diptych: on the one side, the underdeveloped countries, where more than three people out of four are hungry and live in misery, and on the other, those fortunate countries where civilization—although inhuman in some of its aspects—allows the vast majority of its inhabitants to enjoy more than they need.

"I am moved to pity by the crowd", Christ said during his life among us. The cry of his immense love should re-echo still more pityingly today. How has it come about that, in spite of the progress made in the world, there are still so many nations that do not know him? How many among us Christians feel the full tragedy of Christ's anguish? How shall the need to propagate the teaching of the divine Master make itself felt in our times? Even the missions need to be considered today on a worldwide scale. In his Encyclical *Rerum Ecclesiae,* Pius XI quite rightly reminded us of this fact: "The primary reason for the existence of the Church is not the number of its present members, but all mankind. . . . For the Church has no other reason for existence than, by enlarging the Kingdom of Christ throughout the world, to make all men participate in his saving redemption."

To extend the Kingdom of Christ to the whole world has indeed been the primary aim of missionary activity ever since that last command given on Ascension Day. But it has not been the final aim, which still remains the participation of all men in the saving graces of the redemption. And how shall these graces be spread abroad—and through them the King-dom of Christ be extended upon the earth—except primarily by the prodigal manifestation of the vast charity of Christ which is revealed above all in the alleviation of the miseries of men? But to make the love God bears us known only in material forms is not the sole aim of the missions: "Go, then, and make disciples of all nations", Jesus said to his apostles: the implanting of the faith among pagans and the organization of autochthonous Churches in all the countries of the world is the final aim of missionary activity and its success will be shown by its progressive and ultimately complete disappearance.

But if the population of the world is, as we have seen, growing at a rate hitherto inconceivable, we are compelled to admit that the Catholic religion is not being propagated at the same rate. Between 1883 and 1956, the population of Asia and Indonesia grew by 640 million individuals, but the number of Catholics increased by only 23 million (36 per thousand), that of Africa by 120 million, but only by 18 million Catholics (15 per hundred)—and yet the number of African Catholics increased more than sevenfold! In Oceania, where the total growth has been 10 million people, there are $2\frac{1}{2}$ million new Catholics (a quarter—the same proportion as in Europe). But it has been in America that the extension of Catholicism has been the most spectacular: 142 million have been baptized in three-quarters of a century, out of a total growth in population of 250 million. For the world as a whole the total has been scarcely more than 260 million for an increase in population of 1,312 million (barely one-fifth). In the course of the last thirty years, the average yearly increase in the number of baptized has totalled about six million, although separated Christians have also increased by about the same amount and Islam counts 24 million new initiates every year—about four times as many. It cannot be contested that one of the chief reasons—if not the most important single reason—for this lagging behind is the shortage of priests, the lack of workers for the harvest. Although there is in the world about one priest for every thousand baptized Christians, they are very unevenly distributed. Out of the approximately 375,000 priests preaching in the world,

51,000 are in France and only 30,000 in all the mission countries together. In 1948, there were no more in the whole of China than there were in the single diocese of Malines. In Asia, there is, on the average, one priest for 95,000 souls, and in Africa and Oceania, one for 15,000 inhabitants. Yet, despite this shortage of missionary workers, the missions have perhaps never shown as much activity as in our times. In any case, they now show a number of new characteristics which make them unique.

It is customary—and right—to see the beginning of the modern era in missions in the creation of the Sacred Congregation of Propaganda by Gregory XV in 1622. But in fact, although certain nineteenth-century pontiffs showed particular solicitude for the missions (Leo XII and, especially, Gregory XVI and Pius IX), it is to Leo XIII that we today owe our understanding of the fact that the true problems facing the Church, like those facing the world, span the globe. At the end of a terrible war, which had been for him a real Calvary, Benedict XV tried to rescue the missions from nationalistic particularism. Pius XI, by consecrating the first native bishops in 1923, proclaimed the equality of all the children of God. Finally, Pius XII, by proclaiming throughout his pontificate, and especially in his memorable Christmas Message for 1945, the supra-national nature of the Church, succeeded in modelling a new face for the new Church-on-the-March by making a Chinese, an Armenian and a Hindu cardinals. John XXIII, in his coronation sermon, returned to a saying of Pius XI, stating that he was going to give his whole care to the missions "the first, if not indeed the only care of the Roman Pontiff". And continuing the tradition of his glorious predecessor, he raised a Japanese and an African prelate to the cardinalate.

Such, reduced to their main outlines, are the special characteristics of modern missions that we aim to deal with in this short book. After looking at the new conditions governing missionary work, we shall glance briefly at missionary personnel. Next we shall ask ourselves the question "What is a missionary country and how is it organized?" and shall study the various aspects of missionary activity. Finally, after a short world tour around present-day Catholic missions, we shall look at the problems that have arisen for the missions as a result of the political evolution of the world since the last war.

CHAPTER I

SPECIAL CHARACTERISTICS OF MODERN MISSIONS

Unquestionably missions today are not what they were fifty years ago. Essentially, they differ in two main characteristics: first, missionary theory might seem new to uninformed minds, but in fact expresses what the Holy See has laid down in past centuries but adapted to modern techniques; second, there is an increase in missionary personnel—an increase so marked that it would not be going too far to call it revolutionary, debased as that word has become in our days.

It is these two aspects of the contemporary missionary activity that we are going to study first.

PAPAL TEACHING ABOUT THE MISSIONS

In less than half a century four pontiffs have succeeded to the Chair of St Peter who will go down in history as being among the greatest of the missionary popes. They are Benedict XV (1914–22), Pius XI (1922–39), Pius XII (1939–58) and John XXIII. In four remarkably rich and full documents these four popes have, as it were, set out the charter of modern missions.

This of course has not been the first time that the papacy

has taken the initiative in missionary activity. As early as the beginning of the sixth century St Gregory the Great personally organized the mission of the monk Augustine whom he had charged with the evangelization of England, and a hundred and forty years later it was with the support and under the instructions of the Holy See that St Boniface set out on the spiritual conquest of the Germanies. In the seventeenth century, Gregory XV, in founding the Sacred Congregation *De Propaganda Fide* (1622), confirmed that the spreading of the word of God was the special concern of the Vicar of Christ and, thirty years later, Alexander VII, in the famous Instruction of 1659, laid the foundations of pontifical missionary doctrine as we understand it today. Unfortunately, events in the history of the Church made it impossible for the Holy See to develop a systematic policy for the missions before the twentieth century. This systematic policy is therefore now based on four Encyclicals which complement one another in a remarkable way and are a faithful reflection of the eternal mind and activity of the Church; in them is preserved enough flexibility to enable their teaching to be adapted in every age to local needs and customs. In a word, their teaching is both general and universal: that is, it is Catholic.

Maximum illud (Benedict XV, November 30th, 1919)

In a world exhausted by an inhuman war and dreaming of universal brotherhood, the Apostolic Letter *Maximum illud* burst on Catholics like a clap of thunder out of a clear sky. In it the pope expressed his "sorrowing surprise" at the thought that in spite of all the efforts and zeal that had been displayed there were still a thousand million heathen living "in darkness and the shadow of death". It was, he thought, his duty to support the initiative that had been taken "to advance and sustain foreign missions" and to outline the most effective means of sharing in that advance. Hence the

Letter goes on to develop three points that the pontiff considered essential conditions for the progress of missionary work: these were, the duties of the head of a mission, the duties of the missionary and the duties of the Christian world.

He enjoined heads of missions, "bishops, or vicars or prefects apostolic" to be above all the soul of their mission, a vigilant father to all, continually exhorting their fellow-workers to do yet better, and never to be satisfied with results already achieved. What is needed, he said, is continual advance, without either truce or rest, the constant creation of new stations and residences "which will grow into so many seats of new vicariates and prefectures, into which the mission should be divided as soon as opportunities allow".

The head of a mission should continually increase the number of his co-workers, even by appealing to other missionary institutes, especially to those religious foundations whose function it is to run schools, orphanages, hospitals and hospices. He should take the greatest interest in making frequent contacts with his neighbours, for

an efficient head of a mission does not lock himself up within his own limits, as though any other interests outside these were foreign to him. . . . As a matter of fact, there are many interests common to the whole country, which obviously can only be negotiated in common. Besides this, it would be to the greatest profit of the missions were the various heads to gather at stated times for discussion and mutual encouragement.

Finally, the head of a mission must unreservedly give his whole attention to the formation of a native clergy, so that they may as soon as possible become fit to govern the local Church. The pope had to admit that there existed a "regrettable situation": "there is something defective or lacking in the education hitherto given to missionary clergy."

There are still countries where the Catholic faith has been preached for several centuries, but where you will find no indigenous clergy, except of an inferior kind; [it is] sad to think that there are nations who have fully seen the light of the Gospel, have reached such a degree of civilization as to possess men distinguished in every department of secular knowledge; who for many centuries have come under the salutary influence of the Gospel and the Church, and have yet been able to produce neither bishops to rule them, nor priests to direct them.

The first care in this field was therefore to be the foundation of regional seminaries, given their statutes by the Sacred Congregation for Propaganda.

To all missionaries, Benedict XV gives certain fatherly counsels to help them gain the greatest possible success in their apostolate. Above all else, he said, the missionary must avoid the nationalism which has done so much damage to the missions during the recent conflict. "Forget thy people and thy father's house", the Psalmist said, and the pope added: "The mission entrusted to you is more important by far than human interests", and then, more precisely still: "Remember that you are not to propagate the kingdom of men, but that of Christ; that you are not to enrol citizens into any country of this world, but that of the next." Any such activity would quickly be sensed by the native population, and would very soon become suspect to them. For the same reason the missionary should be completely untouched by thoughts of material profit for himself or for his homeland.

Anyone who sets out to win other souls for Christ should have a care of a completely different order: that of preparing himself well for his task. It is a fundamental error to say that he does not need much skill to preach Christ to savages for he will often have to reply to very perplexing questions and objections. Hence he needs to know doctrine extremely thoroughly—as the Protestants know it. With this end in view, a specific and scientific course of instruction for missionaries was to be brought into being at Propaganda's Urban College. In addition, the pope wrote, the missionary should be in possession of the fundamental elements of the languages of the peoples among whom he is to be called on to work. The ability to speak to them "with facility and accuracy" is necessary to ensure for him the most perfect fruits of his preaching.

Lastly, the example of a holy life—humility, obedience, chastity, piety, goodness, patience and, above all, absolute trust in God—will allow him to begin his work without fear of the obstacles which may face him.

But, the pope says, missionary work in a pagan country is not the affair only of certain individuals. It is the duty of the whole Christian world, which should help it forward first by its prayers; then, by supplying it with priests, for missionary personnel are in notoriously short supply; and lastly by sending them supplies, for the need had grown with the war. What was sent, the pope said, was to go by the channels of the Pontifical Mission Aid Societies: the Association for the Propagation of the Faith, the Society of the Holy Childhood (the aim of which is to ensure the baptism of heathen children in danger of death), the Society of St Peter the Apostle (for the training of a native clergy in the missions), and the Missionary Union of the Clergy (which the pope wished to see established in all the dioceses of the Christian world).

Such were Benedict XV's instructions. It would not be right to suggest that his Letter sketched the likeness of an ideal missionary, and his interdictions were only a true catalogue of conditions then current. But we are compelled to admit that they were by no means exceptional, for a few weeks later the pope returned to certain aspects of the problem in the Instruction *Quo efficacius* (January 6th, 1920), which recalled that missionaries should beware of wanting to spread the language of their homeland among a native population, even in mission schools, and should, on the contrary, learn the local language so as to be able to preach, teach the catechism and exhort and hear confessions; that they should not introduce the laws and customs of their homelands, but only those in force in the universal Church; should abandon any idea of opening a way among the peoples entrusted to them for political penetration by their native countries and preach the obedience of the faithful to public authorities and to the laws "provided they are honest, and not inimical to religion"; lastly, that they should ask their superiors for permission to publish any political work or journal and devote missionary publications solely to extending the Kingdom of God, and not to the aggrandizement of their own nation.

Benedict XV, then, thought that nationalism was repugnant to the spirit of missionary work and that its disappearance was an essential condition of the missionary renewal indispensable to the progress of the universal Church. Immediately on his accession, his successor Pius XI, who is generally thought of as the restorer of missionary work among the heathen—for all too often the importance of the instructions given by his predecessor is forgotten—declared his anxiety to do what seemed most urgent: that is, strengthen his effective forces: "it is our intention to face up to the needs of the missions as a whole according to a rational and methodical plan", he declared at the time of the transfer of the Association for the Propagation of the Faith to Rome (May 3rd, 1922). A month later, on the occasion of the third centenary of the Sacred Congregation of Propaganda, he said in his sermon that in the view of the masses who, in Africa, China and India, were looking for the Word of salvation "the number of workers is insufficient and the methods used are a weak point in the work".

Meanwhile Propaganda addressed a letter to the missionary Orders and Societies (*Lo sviluppo*, May 20th, 1923), to bring into practice the recommendations of *Maximum illud*: it spoke of the study of local languages and customs; the training of a local clergy, which should not be restricted to a rôle auxiliary to that of the missionary, but prepared for its future rôle in the leadership of the local Church; and of the necessity of providing for the training and sending out of colleagues to help the missionary in his many tasks.

Rerum Ecclesiae (Pius XI, February 28th, 1926)

It was into this situation that Pius XI launched his famous Encyclical. Paying solemn homage to his predecessors, he recalled that the help of the Christian world to the missions was a sacred duty demanded by the love of God and charity towards one's neighbour, and that it was a very special duty of priests and bishops to lend their support to it. Then, having laid special stress on the encouragement of missionary vocations, the pope called on all Christians to interest themselves actively in missionary work.

Speaking to the heads of missions, he commanded them to work with all their powers for the formation of a native clergy, priests first of all, but also religious of both sexes and catechists. Referring to *Maximum illud* he said very clearly that it was his intention that an indigenous clergy should be brought into being everywhere: "From the fact that the Roman Pontiff has entrusted to you and to your helpers the task of preaching the Christian religion to the pagan nations, you ought not to conclude that the rôle of the native clergy is merely one of assisting the missionaries in minor matters and merely completing their work".

The formation of a native clergy is, moreover, in keeping with the tradition of the apostles. Peoples have a natural right to pastors of their own race and country, the pope said, and it is in the Church's own interest that they should have them, although the missionary whose task it would be to train a local clergy in his mission would have to go before it and

carry the Gospel to peoples who did not yet know it. Recalling also the Apostolic Letter of his predecessor, Pius XI,
whose vision was extraordinarily prophetic of coming events,
stated:

> If owing to a war or political upheavals there is a change of
> government in some missionary territory, and the request is
> made or a law passed that the foreign missions of a certain
> country must leave: suppose again, a more likely case, that the
> native population, raised to a higher degree of culture and
> political development, in order to gain its freedom wants to
> drive out of their territory all governors, armed forces and
> missionaries belonging to the occupying foreign power, and
> that it cannot do so otherwise than by force. What then, we
> ask, would be the disaster that would threaten the Church
> throughout all that territory, unless full provision had been
> made for the needs of the Christian populace by a network of
> native priests throughout the whole country?

Pius XI therefore ordered all heads of missions in the field
of their apostolate to open regional seminaries in which
autochthonous priests might be trained, equal in knowledge
and powers with the missionaries. What was needed, he
wrote, was a clerical élite, for it was destined to lead the
local church. At the same time, it was necessary to bring
into being indigenous congregations of monks and nuns who
could be called on to replace the brothers and sisters from
overseas, although the pope did not want to suggest that
natives should be forbidden to enter existing orders. At the
same time it was necessary, the pope said, to guide native
populations towards the contemplative life by the foundation
of monasteries like that of the Trappists in the Vicariate of
Pekin, which was very successful because it held no less than
a hundred religious, all of them Chinese.

Nor should we pass over in silence another point, which is
most important for the propagation of the Faith; namely, the
importance of multiplying the number of catechists—whether

they be chosen from Europeans, or preferably from the natives, who may help the missionaries, particularly by instructing catechumens and preparing them for baptism.

It is not necessary to speak of the qualities which should adorn these catechists that they may be able to draw the infidels to Christ, more by the example of their lives than by word. And do you, Venerable Brethren, and Beloved Sons, fervently resolve to educate them with all solicitude, in order that they may learn well the Christian doctrine, and that, in teaching it, they may be able to adapt themselves to the character and intelligence of their catechism classes, in which work their success will be in exact proportion to the intimate knowledge they have of the mentality of the natives.

Here he was in fact dealing with the organization of missionary work. He next outlines strategy, the conduct of missionary operations: first of all, it is necessary to effect a complete penetration of the territory entrusted to the mission, and next to win the hearts of peoples by practising a practical charity, by caring for the sick, as Jesus did, and like him, training small children. The missionary must beware of spectacular and expensive buildings and be able to feel content with a humble chapel and instead increase the number of the works (schools, dispensaries, hospitals) "lack of which you should not tolerate anywhere". It is important not to neglect the nobility and ruling classes for "experience teaches us that when once the leaders of the people have been converted to Christianity, the ordinary people follow closely in their footsteps". The final aim of all these activities will naturally be to prepare for the end of the missionary stage, which will see the division of present mission territories and the creation of local bishoprics, for missionaries must "remember that they have not received their portion of the Lord's vineyard by a kind of private title in perpetuity. Rather they hold it at the will of the Apostolic See."

In other documents Pius XI on several occasions returns

to the instructions of *Rerum Ecclesiae* and the teaching of his predecessor, notably in the Letter *Ab ipsis* (June 15th, 1926) addressed to the Chinese Church, at that time accused of political activity. The pope recalled that the Church is Catholic: that is, that "it embraces all nations, that the divine Will of Christ its Founder forbids it any internal distinctions of race or class", that missionaries are not sent by governments, but by God himself, and that they should not concern themselves in temporal affairs, but that their primary task is the training of native priests to guide the destinies of their own Church.

Evangelii praecones (Pius XII, June 2nd, 1951)

It was not without good reason that Cardinal Pacelli, when called on March 2nd, 1939 to succeed Pius XI, took the regnal name of his predecessor. Moreover, he showed immediately that he wished to continue his missionary activity by raising a Malagasi and an African to the episcopate two months after his coronation. In his Encyclical *Summi Pontificatus* (October 20th, 1939), and his Christmas Message of 1945, he returned very forcefully to the guiding concept of missionary activity as conceived by Pius XI, the catholicity of the Church. He gave it singular reinforcement by proclaiming the *supra-national* character of the work of Christ. In order to facilitate missionary activity, he did not hesitate to establish diplomatic relations with non-Catholic countries such as China, India, Indonesia, Liberia, Pakistan, Japan and Ethiopia. He authorized certain missions to use local languages in worship, to make easier communion of thought between celebrant and congregation. He greatly increased the number of native bishops in missionary countries. But above all he celebrated the twenty-fifth anniversary of *Rerum Ecclesiae* in a particularly striking manner by publishing the Encyclical *Evangelii praecones* on June 2nd, 1951.

After having drawn up the balance-sheet of twenty-five

years' missionary work, he stated the true position regarding missionary affairs, touching on principles of conduct for missionaries, the participation of lay people in mission work, the principal activities of missions and the need for respect for everything that was good in the civilization of nations. He ended by recalling the duty of the Christian world to help missions. It is the middle part of this Encyclical which is by far the most important and calls for some explanation of the missionary teaching of Pius XII.

"With a view to promoting still more effectively the work of evangelization by our missionaries and to prevent one drop of their sweat and blood from being shed in vain, we should like here to explain briefly the principles and norms that must guide the zeal and activities of Catholic missionaries." First, the missionary should "consider the country he is going to evangelize as a second fatherland and love it with due charity", his first fatherland being not that of his birth but the Kingdom of God. Consequently, he should seek no material advantage either for the advancement of the interests of his own country or those of his religious institute. He should acquire a large body of religious and profane knowledge: the local tongues, medicine, agriculture, ethnography, history and geography of the country where he has to exercise his apostolate, so that he may be well advised on everything. Finally, he should not forget that the fundamental aim of his mission is not only the raising up of new Christians but also the formation of a native clergy and the preparation of a local hierarchy, "to extend the Church into new districts in such a way that it may enroot itself ever more deeply in them, and that after it has developed there it may be able, as soon as possible afterwards, to live there and flourish without the aid of missionary works".

The participation of lay people in missionary work is equally a pre-condition of its success. Since the beginning of the Church and throughout its history, lay people have participated in the labour of the apostolate. Today, in missionary countries, this work is necessary even apart from the activities of catechists. Indeed, only lay people are qualified to lead branches of Catholic Action and youth organizations.

The mission must also carry its activity into various other fields: first, that of teaching, so as to form an élite who, because they keep the stamp received in school, even if they do not go as far as conversion, will thus be preserved from the inauspicious influences of non-Catholics and Communists. Moreover, this stamp should be reinforced by that of the Press. In this direction, however, there is still much to be done. Social and public health work can also bear very rich fruits for the apostolate. The episcopate—and this rôle is peculiarly its own—should watch to see that justice is done, for charity is not enough; and, in order to ensure that all the obligations of the missionary state are fulfilled, bishops should not hesitate to call in the help of specialist institutions. They should imitate fully established dioceses, the pope added, where "additional priests, brothers, and sisters from different religious families come in and help the bishop. So, too, in the missions do not hesitate to summon to your aid as your co-workers missionaries who are not of your own religious family, whether they be priests or belong to lay institutes."

Finally Pius XII laid stress on the need to respect everything that is good in the civilization of pagan nations, as the Church has done from the beginning. What is needed is not destruction, but the grafting "of a good scion upon the wild stock that it may bear a crop of more delicious fruit".[1] The Gospel will be more readily heard if the traditional environment of the native is respected.

In this Encyclical, Pius XII frequently alludes to his earlier observations. Until his death he never stopped showing great

[1] See Select Bibliography at the end of this volume for source of translated extracts of papal documents.

solicitude for the missions and claiming for them the help of the whole Christian world. In another Encyclical (*Fidei donum*, April 21st, 1957), which is devoted to the situation facing Catholic missions in Africa, and which we shall study later, he calls for what is in truth a general mobilization of the Christian world in the service of the missions.

Notice how wonderfully the three great documents we have just briefly summarized complement one another. All three insist on "denationalization" and disinterestedness from the missionary, the abandonment of all exclusiveness over missionary territory and the necessity of collaboration between different institutes, and the common duty of faithful, clergy and episcopate in helping the missions by participating actively in the pontifical missionary societies or in the Missionary Union of the Clergy.

In *Rerum Ecclesiae*, Pius XI strongly emphasized the responsibility of the Vicar of Christ with regard to the missions. The evangelization of those outside the Church is his special duty; it is for him to direct it, distribute the funds it needs, and tax the established episcopate to raise such funds. Pius XI also made innovations regarding missionary personnel by sanctioning the establishment of the contemplative Orders in mission countries. In addition, he laid stress on traditional and complete training for native clergy and on the need to bring into being educational schemes covering not only elementary but also higher grades.

In *Evangelii praecones*, Pius XII laid even greater stress on the primary importance of education in all its forms, especially technical education. He defined the rôle of Catholic Action in mission countries, called for the association of the native laity with mission work, and authorized a considerable increase in activities concerned with public health and welfare because, as he said in the Letter *Perlibenti equidem* to the prefect of Propaganda (August 16th, 1950) "the romance of the apostolate is no longer enough".

There, then, is the summary of the broad guiding principles of the contemporary apostolate. While remaining wholly faithful to the tradition of the Church, it abandons some of the ideas which formerly found acceptance, especially that of the supreme importance of the number of baptisms administered and of the exclusive rights of a particular missionary institute in a given field of activity.

But, it might have been asked at the time of the death of Pius XII, does this programme constitute the unvarying charter of the missions? We already know the answer to this question. At the time of his coronation, John XXIII declared that "the care of the Roman Pontiff—truly his first, if not his only one" was to bring into the fold the sheep who are outside it. And to mark the fortieth anniversary of *Maximum illud* he returned to, and defined more precisely, certain aspects of the problem in his Encyclical *Princeps pastorum* (November 28th, 1959), which is in no way less important than the instructions of his three glorious predecessors.

Princeps pastorum (John XXIII, November 28th, 1959)

After having recalled that at the request of Benedict XV he had devoted four years of his life to the Work of Propagation of the Faith, he defines the Encyclical *Maximum illud* as "a cry of spiritual awakening to new and peaceful conquests for the Kingdom of God". As an outline of the present situation he adds: "Since then, over a period of forty years, missionary activity has become ever more intense and a new fact of the highest importance has come further to enrich the already splendid progress of the missions: the development of the autochthonous hierarchy and clergy. . . . This has always been the programme of the S. Congregation of Propaganda. However, it must be said that it was the Letter *Maximum illud* that brought into the full light of day—as it had never been brought before—the importance and urgency of the problem."

Pius XI and Pius XII renewed Benedict XV's call, and the results have been encouraging: many areas have passed beyond the missionary state and now possess their own hierarchies. The fraternal collaboration of local clergy and missionaries from other lands is still necessary because of the magnitude of the task to be performed.

The training of a local clergy, however, poses a number of problems. Spiritual training is of primary importance in the formation of young clergy, for, knowing well as they do the mentality and aspirations of their fellow-countrymen, they "find themselves wonderfully fitted to inculcate the Faith into their hearts". Hence the necessity of increasing the number of native seminaries. The education of a native priest should be adapted to the environment in which he will have to preach the Gospel, because surroundings too cut off from the world would on leaving the seminary lay him open to the dangers of meeting with "difficulties with the people or the educated classes". Any such risk of being cut off could not but prejudice his mission. His education should be given him from the point of view of the responsibilities and spirit of initiative required of the future leaders of a native Church. From this point of view, it is clear that it is necessary to make use of local outlooks and standards. Hence the need for more profound missiological studies in missionaries' seminaries. Furthermore, it is necessary to penetrate deeply into the educated classes, following the example of Matteo Ricci, the glorious forerunner of modern missions. With this end in view, it is necessary to bring into being centres of study and teaching of Christian doctrine open to a wide public. It is of course not possible to do everything everywhere, but every opportunity must be grasped, and it must be realized that one sows and another reaps (cf. John 4. 37). Where social work and welfare are concerned, it is necessary to act with the greatest prudence, in such a way as never to imperil apostolic activity. Missionaries should therefore restrict themselves to those works that are necessary, can be easily maintained or quickly completed and can, as quickly as possible, be entrusted to the natives, so that missionaries may devote themselves exclusively to the teaching of doctrine. Lastly, the local clergy should not be instructed only in their own problems, but also in the interest, situation and vicissitudes of the universal Church. They should also be trained in that spirit of universal charity which is the manifestation of Catholic unity.

Alluding to the winning of political liberties by numerous nations, John XXIII exhorts native priests never to forget that the doctrine of Christ embraces all men with the same love. They must therefore work for the real welfare of all men. Besides, being universal, the Church can never allow any partiality or form of nationalism.

John XXIII then defines the rôle of the laity in the missions. The aim of the missions is in fact not merely the administration of baptism or the entering of names on registers; it is the training of Christians of deep faith, prepared to assume their responsibilities in the life and future of the Church. It is for the clergy to make the laity aware of their responsibilities, and in order to do so to inculcate in them absolute love for God in the totality of their actions and life. The laity should, then, be witnesses to the truth not only in their words, but also in their whole lives. Their charity must be real and, as St Paul said, without hypocrisy. The concrete manifestation of their charity will consist in their contribution to the material needs of the community. "It is a good thing for the autochthonous faithful to grow accustomed to spontaneously maintaining, in so far as they are able, their churches and institutions and the clergy who are wholly devoted to them. It does not greatly matter if this contribution is not very great. The essential thing is that it should be tangible evidence of a Christian conscience truly alive."

So that missionaries may more easily attain these ends, the

pope ends his Encyclical by giving some instructions regarding the apostolate of the laity in the missions. It will, he said, be necessary to train ever more catechists "the right arms of the Lord's labourers". To give effective aid to the hierarchy, it needs lay people in large numbers to swell the ranks of Catholic Action in all its forms. "We can never overemphasize the necessity of adapting this form of the apostolate as necessary to local conditions and needs. The most important problem is, then, the training of lay readers for these movements, who should "give the fullest proof of a really serious and superior Christian formation, both intellectually and morally". The natural place for such formation would be Christian schools, but a plan for the training of leaders of Catholic Action can only "with difficulty find a place in scholastic programmes"; thence arises the necessity of having recourse to schemes operating outside the schools. It is equally necessary, in the face of the independence movements that have manifested themselves among so many peoples, to direct Catholics towards public office, so that the destiny of nations may be entrusted to good men; the rôle of Catholics might be of special importance in the organization of schools, social welfare and labour. The scientific and technical help of nations which have long been Christian should be given to new nations as a token of charity.

Such then is the most recent pontifical teaching. The plan of the work has been laid down. We must now look at the forces whose task it is to carry it out.

MISSIONARY PERSONNEL

It appears from pontifical teaching that missionary personnel may be divided into two categories of workers in the apostolate: local clergy and those who have come from other countries (who, as an aid to simplification, we shall call "the Europeans", although the proportion of missionaries who have come from the United States and Canada is not negligible). One point must be made: although the "Europeans" all belong to Congregations of religious or to missionary institutes, a very large majority of autochthonous clergy are secular priests. Methods of recruitment and training naturally differ from one category to another, but all have a common aim and, with their one love for God and man in common, do identical work.

European missionaries

Although missions had their beginnings in the apostolic age itself, it must be recognized that their systematic development began with the opening of the colonial era. The Portuguese and Spaniards, when they built up their colonial empire at the beginning of the sixteenth century, sent missionaries from their homelands to convert the indigenous populations, but forbade religious of other nations admission to their possessions. Thence arose the *Patronato*, which was still operative a short time ago in Portuguese possessions. In fact, foreign missionaries could exercise their apostolate in Hispanic territories overseas, if they had first taken care to train in Lisbon or Spain and ask permission of the sovereign. This was done, for example, by those Italian Jesuits who, as early as the end of the sixteenth century, started the spiritual conquest of India and China. An analogous system, that of the Protectorate, was established in the middle of the nineteenth century in the Near and Far East for the benefit of all European missionaries by France. Such a system allowed the protecting nation to give the Holy See the right of supervision over the missions. In the years preceding the war of 1914–18, the colonial nations exercised a very jealous patronage in their overseas possessions and practically forbade admission to their colonies of missionaries coming from any other state.

It was against this interference on the part of governments in the affairs of the Church that Benedict XV was reacting when, in *Maximum illud*, he ordered missionaries to "denationalize" themselves. Hence today we see religious of different nationalities working side by side in the same district to spread their common homeland, the Kingdom of God.

In 1959 there were about 28,000 missionaries. Statistics compiled in 1953 listed 24,974, of whom 14,151 were of European origin, 1,824 of American origin and 8,999 came from the mission territories. By country of origin they included:

3,505 French	1,332 Italian	709 Canadian
2,289 Belgian	847 German	549 English
2,229 Dutch	829 American	362 Swiss
2,001 Irish	779 Spanish	

Comparison of this set of figures[2] showing missionaries by nationality with a similar set of statistics published in 1933 shows that the number of French missionaries is practically unchanged (3,373 in 1933; 3,505 in 1953). The same is true for the Italians (1,251 in 1933; 1,332 in 1953). The number of Germans (954 in 1933; 847 in 1953) and Spaniards (860 in 1933; 779 in 1953) has decreased. By contrast, the number of Belgians (1,106 in 1933; 2,289 in 1953) and of Dutch missionaries (941 in 1933; 2,229 in 1953) has doubled, while that of English (241 in 1933; 549 in 1953), Swiss (159 in 1933; 362 in 1953) and American (373 in 1933; 829 in 1953) has increased two and a half times. The number of Canadians (285 as against 709) has tripled and that of the Irish (314 as against 2001) has increased sixfold.

A comparison of the number of missionary priests with the total number of priests in each country shows that Holland has become Europe's leading missionary country, with one-fifth of its priests engaged on missionary work. Then come Ireland (16 per cent), Belgium (12 per cent), Switzerland (7 per cent), France and Great Britain (6 per

[2] These figures, compiled by Fr Schorer, were quoted by Fr Adrien Bouffard in *Perspectives sur le monde* (Quebec, 1957).

cent), Canada (5·5 per cent), Germany (3 per cent), Spain (2·5 per cent), Italy (2 per cent) and lastly the United States of America (1·8 per cent).

The total of about 16,000 "European" missionaries listed above are divided among ninety institutes and Congregations, thirty-two of them founded by natives of France. Fifty-four of them have been founded since 1800 and sixteen of these since the beginning of this century. But in 1950 only six of them had more than a thousand members in missionary countries: these were the Jesuits (3,973), the White Fathers (1,797), the Franciscans (1,774), the Salesians of St John Bosco (1,374), the Oblates of Mary Immaculate (1,222) and the Holy Ghost Fathers (1,197). Thus, among those six institutes alone there are to be found two-thirds of the European missionary personnel. Nine other Congregations have an effective apostolic force of between 500 and 1,000 members: these are the Society of the Divine Word, the Missionaries of the Immaculate Heart of Mary (the Scheutists), the Capuchins, the Paris Foreign Missionary Society (*Missions Étrangères de Paris*), the Redemptorists, the Dominicans, the Society for African Missions of Lyons, the Society for Foreign Missions of Mill Hill and the Vincentians.

These figures do not include either the Institutes of religious who are not priests,[3] or the innumerable Congregations of nuns, of which a hundred are wholly French—such congregations, to name but a single example, as the Sisters of the Foreign Missions of Muret, who devote themselves to the most wretched of the outcasts of South India.[4]

The most famous of all missionary congregations—perhaps because of its glorious past—is the Society of Jesus. In 1959, the number of its members active in missionary countries was more than 6,000, of whom a third were autochthonous (about 18 per cent of the total number of missionary priests). They

[3] Some institutes are mixed, with both priest-religious and brothers.
[4] See *Ecclesia* (April 1954), n. 61, pp. 71–4.

were divided among sixty-one missionary territories. They conducted five large regional seminaries (Tokyo, Rangoon, Dalat, Port-au-Prince and Tananarive) and two universities (Tokyo and Seoul). In addition, they were teaching in five other universities (Saigon, Bankok, Taipeh, Hong Kong and Manila). They also directed four university colleges at Duala and Tamara (in Morocco), Katmandu (in Nepal—which was still forbidden territory to missions twenty-five years ago) and Singapore. An Indian archbishop and two bishops belong to the society, as well as two Chinese bishops (now expelled), and two vicars apostolic in Indonesia and a third in Mexico. In Africa, eight territories have been entrusted to them; in America they have been called to the evangelization of the Indian tribes in the Rocky Mountains, Mexico, Colombia, Ecuador, Peru, Paraguay and the Matto Grosso. Remember, too, that in China before 1949 there were 910 of them, of whom 250 were Chinese, and that their mission in Shanghai (with the University of the Dawn, the College of St Ignatius, the interdiocesan major seminary and the observatory of Zi Ka-Wei) suffered particularly by persecution, the Rector of the College of St Ignatius, Fr Beda Tsang, having been martyred.

The *Missions Étrangères de Paris* has, since its foundation in 1664, devoted itself especially to the training of native clergy, and in the year following its foundation it founded in Siam the first native seminary in the Far East. Between that time and 1925, it trained more than 2,750 Asian priests.

The White Fathers, the spiritual sons of Cardinal Lavigerie, numbered 2,768 in 1957. For a long time they were exclusively French, but today they include members of thirty different nationalities and for the first time their superior is of Dutch nationality. At the present time they number 936 Frenchmen, 652 Belgians, 491 Dutchmen, 406 Canadians, 265 Germans, 149 Britons, 106 Swiss, etc., and we must not forget the ten Africans. They are divided among forty missions and have charge of twenty-five million souls. In the single year 1955, they performed 310,000 baptisms and instructed a million catechumens. In Ruanda, they have, by the Holy Father's orders, had to limit the number of baptisms in order to avoid the creation of priestless communities of Christians.

The Congregation of the Holy Ghost, founded in 1840 by Fr Libermann, has, since its foundation, been devoted to the evangelization of black Africa. It has played an extremely important part in the building up of an African Church in a French milieu. At present there are several autochthonous prelates in the former states of the French colonial empire.

The African Missions of Lyons, founded in 1856 with the same aim, also show a flattering balance-sheet. Its missionary activity extends over some 480,000 square miles, with 26,000,000 inhabitants, of whom 1,200,000 are baptized and 250,000 are catechumens. The Society has twenty-one bishops and 1,621 members, of whom 1,258 are priests, 264 are admitted seminarians and 99 coadjutor brothers. Among these there are 112 African priests and one archbishop, Mgr Gantin, an ex-student of the major seminary of Uidah (Dahomey).

It now becomes obvious why in the light of such fruitful work pontifical instructions, and especially the Encyclical *Rerum Ecclesiae,* have insisted on the necessity of collaboration between the various institutes in one and the same district. Henceforward, as far as evangelization is concerned there will be no more "hunting preserves, no more apostolic capitalism. The needs of souls will come before everything."[5]

Native clergy

Alexander VII in 1659, Gregory XVI in 1845, Pius IX in 1868 and Leo XIII in 1893 all called for the training of native priests and Benedict XV deplored the fact that results

[5] Fr J.-Em. Janot, S.J., in *Rythmes du Monde* (1951), n. 2, p. 112.

were still inadequate. We have seen with what prophetic spirit Pius XI set out the grounds for the urgent indigenization of the missionary Churches. But it should not be thought that in this matter the Church was guided by a policy of mere opportunism. The Holy See has always believed that the future of the Church in mission territories depends above all else on its being taken over by the people of those territories themselves.

Of course, the training of a native clergy does not proceed entirely without difficulty, for they need to reach the same standard as all other Catholic priests if the very office of priest is not to be debased. This is why pontifical instructions forbid any indulgence in connection with moral or disciplinary regulations. It is also necessary for a native priest to be armed adequately with the doctrine of the catholicity of the Church, so that he is able to resist any temptation to schism. Recent events in China have shown how pressing this need is. His devotion and zeal must be unfaltering, for pastoral tasks will be entrusted to him, while the onus of missionary tasks will fall on the "foreigners". In this way, the foreigners, being relieved of pastoral cares, will be able to penetrate more deeply into the territory entrusted to them.

It cannot be denied that the indigenization of missionary Churches corresponds to a psychological need. In a period when all the nations of Asia and Africa have suddenly found themselves in the grip of nationalism, Christianity, in spite of its supernatural character, is in danger of seeming a foreign religion. Only native priests can effectively refute this untruth and give the Church integral stability within the life of the new nations. The course of this evolution, however, may vary considerably from one district to another, according to the level of civilization or evolution of the population.

In 1925, there were 4,516 indigenous priests; in 1954 there were 13,700 and 16,800 seminarians. Over a period of forty years progress was even more spectacular, as can be seen from the figures for Asia and Africa:

	1918	1957
Asia	919	5,553
Africa	90	1,811

The first seven native bishops were consecrated in 1929. By 1959, the number of sees entrusted to local hierarchies had grown to ninety-eight. Moreover, between June 30th, 1959, and June 30th, 1960, John XXIII named fourteen new missionary bishops, of whom six were Africans and two Madagascan, so bringing to twenty-two the number of natives raised to the episcopate since his coronation.[6] Neither should we forget the recent nomination to the College of Cardinals of the archbishop of Tokyo and of an African bishop, Mgr Rugambwa of Tanganyika, who was the first Prince of the Church of Negro blood.

There are now mission countries in which the number of native priests is larger—sometimes much larger—than the number of foreign missionaries. Thus the proportion of local clergy reaches 58 per cent in South Korea and is more than 60 per cent in India and 80 per cent in Vietnam. Although the percentage of local priests is as low as twenty-three in Japan, it should be noted that all the dioceses of that country have been entrusted to Japanese prelates. Notice too that autochthonous clergy represent more than 30 per cent of the total of priests in Ruanda and more than 20 per cent in both Madagascar and the Cameroons, 14 per cent in Indonesia, but less than 10 per cent in both Senegal and Southern Rhodesia, and 5 per cent in the Sudan and Guinea.

But the best criterion of proof that a mission Church has attained its majority is surely the organization of national councils. The first of these ever to be held took place in

[6] On June 30th, 1960, there were, by the author's calculation, a total of a hundred and thirty-six autochthonous bishops.

Vietnam in 1934. Australia's first national council was in 1937 (it should moreover be noticed that Australia is today thought of as a missionary country only by a legal fiction). More significant still, perhaps, was the Indian plenarv council that was held at Bangalore from January 6th–13th, 1950: it fully demonstrated the great vitality of the Indian Church for there were present forty-six prelates of whom twenty were Indian, three bishops from the Portuguese possessions (which are subject to the Patriarchate of Lisbon) and sixteen bishops of the Eastern Rite (Syro-Malabar and Syro-Malankar).

Pontifical instructions lay special stress on the training of an indigenous clergy. It is therefore indispensable to establish seminaries in the mission countries. Some were already in being, but they were not enough. Others were created as a result of *Maximum illud* and *Rerum Ecclesiae*, especially in Africa where the results were remarkable. Today there are thirty-eight major seminaries in the continent of Africa: seven in West Africa (three in the former French colonies; two in Ghana; two in Nigeria); eight in Central Africa (four in the Congo; one in Ruanda; one in the Cameroons; one at Brazzaville; one at Fernando Po); eleven in East Africa (one at Nyassa; five in Tanganyika; three in Uganda; two in Kenya); four in North-east Africa (one in Eritrea; two in Ethiopia; one in Egypt); one in Madagascar.

These thirty-eight seminaries are entrusted to eighteen different institutes: the White Fathers and the Holy Ghost Fathers direct more than any others (seven each); then come the Jesuits and the African Missions of Lyons with three each. The Vincentians, the Benedictines and the Mill Hill Fathers and those of the Consolata of Turin each direct two. In thirty years—from 1922 to 1952—the number has increased by twenty-two. The number of students increased during this same period from 189 to 1,185—an increase of almost 525 per cent. It now becomes very obvious why the number of active priests of black race increased sixfold between 1933 and 1954. 1956 saw for the first time the elevation to the episcopate of a White Father of Swiss nationality consecrated by a Negro bishop, Mgr Bigirumwani of Ruanda.

The thorough training of native seminarians deserves our brief attention. For the first attempts (after the somewhat unfortunate endeavours made on the initiative of M. Jahvou-hey) we are indebted to the Holy Ghost Fathers. For long they hesitated about the method to be followed: should men be trained in Europe, or where they were? The first method having given only very poor results, they bravely adopted the second. They certainly experienced many disappoint-ments: difficulties with Latin studies led to loss of many candidates; sickness took a heavy toll of the students; family and tribal surroundings led to many defections. Beginning in 1900, the White Fathers in their turn took up this task. The most encouraging results have been obtained in certain districts of East and Central Africa: in 1933, out of one hundred and fifty black priests, fifty-one were natives of Uganda and twenty-six of Tanganyika. Taking into account the members of major and minor seminaries in 1957, it may be hoped that by 1975 Africa will have more than three thousand native priests.

Special efforts have been made to ensure that the semin-aries produce superior men of irreproachable virtue. En-deavours are made to give black priests an ideal of com-munity life which offers, among other advantages, that of making it possible to entrust to two or three indigenous priests missions which would weigh too heavily on a single man. They may then examine their problems in common and in the majority of cases avoid errors of judgement or apprecia-tion. Moreover, as the spirit of common life imbues the lives of all Africans these methods lead to young African priests being less cut off from their ancestral traditions. A life of this kind also protects the young priest from the dangers of solitude. Special precautions are taken to safeguard respect for the vow of chastity: no woman servant is allowed in a missionary community; no contact is allowed in private between a priest and a woman. These precautions are absolutely necessary in the environment in which the young priest is called to exercise his ministry—an environment wholly impregnated by paganism, where the concept of perpetual celibacy is something completely new—if the witness of exemplary conduct is not to give rise to any ambiguity.

From these short indications it is possible to estimate the quality of the priests so trained. It is not surprising that the élite from among this new clergy has so quickly been adjudged worthy of the episcopate.

But what may seem even more surprising is the success of the contemplative Orders among native peoples in certain missionary territories. In *Rerum Ecclesiae* Pius XI charged the missions to implant in their provinces "that most austere tradition, the contemplative life" and cited the remarkable example of the Trappist foundation in the vicariate of Pekin. This has not been the only success in this direction. There is, for example, the foundation in Morocco of one of the most spiritually precious of all Christianity's places, the monastery of Tiumliline, where the Cross meets Islam, whence, with the help of God, there may one day come deeper mutual understanding between the world's two greatest religions and, perhaps—who can say?—the grounds on which they may draw closer together or be reconciled.

Similarly the Benedictines have a foundation in Katanga. There are Trappist and Dominican monasteries in the Congo and Japan, and we have recently read of the ordination of the first Congolese Dominican. The Poor Clares have a foundation in Tanganyika. Three Carmels have been founded in Ruanda and the Cameroons, and there also several Cameronian postulants have recently made their perpetual vows. But what are we to think of the Trappistines in Japan? This order, which enforces the most severe rule in the religious world—absolute silence, total abstinence from all meat, and rising at three in the morning—has succeeded in establishing four foundations in the Land of the Rising Sun—more than in either Spain or Ireland. The first convent of Japanese Trappistines was founded in 1898. Today the four convents have a total of four hundred nuns coming from every level of Japanese society.

CHAPTER II

WHAT IS A MISSIONARY COUNTRY?

Taking the word mission in its widest sense, it could be said that the whole world is a missionary country, even those countries where Christianity has long been established—even those where the vast majority of the population are practising Catholics. This is why a famous book is entitled *La France, Pays de Mission?* (but notice the question mark).[1] By the very grace of our baptism Christ has sent us (as missionaries) to make his words known to those who do not know him, or do not know him well. By extension, therefore, a people that does not know the teaching of Jesus, or a nation that does not know him well, becomes a missionary country. Does this mean that papal instructions apply to all pagan and schismatic countries? They do not. In the first place, some Encyclicals have been addressed to a country or particular group of countries by name. Among these were the Encyclical *Ad Sinarum gentem* (Pius XII, October 7th, 1954) addressed to the Catholics of China, and the Encyclical *Fidei donum* (Pius XII, April 21st, 1957), which deals with the situation in the Churches of Africa. Thus, to see exactly what a missionary country is, we must seek our information elsewhere.

We have so far envisaged the definition of the word "mission" only in relation to ourselves and those like us: we

[1] English translation: *France Pagan* (London and New York), Sheed and Ward.

have concerned ourselves only with its subjective or personal sense, and neglected its collective meaning. But the whole body of baptized individuals forms a collective organism, a society, the society of the Church. Very rightly we often speak of the mission of the Church when we wish to refer to the task Christ has entrusted to her because she is what she is. It is the Church's duty to fulfil this task everywhere, and especially in pagan countries. This is the meaning we currently give to the word mission—but this meaning of the word is only an expression of a particular aspect of the duty laid on the whole Christian community. When we speak of the "mission" devolving on this or that particular Order or Institute, we are no longer speaking of the office, but of the organ performing the office, the organ through which the office is fulfilled. Finally, there is yet another derivative meaning given to the word mission: its most common use today is as the definition of a particular district where the missionary office is being fulfilled—as, for example, in the phrase "the Congo mission".

In fact, missionary activity, the office of the Church, is not an end in itself, but is a means to a particular end: to bring all men to the benefit of the graces of the redemption by the extension of the Kingdom of Christ throughout the world, as our Lord commanded his Apostles to do. In our own times, this missionary office has devolved on the pope. Recent popes —Benedict XV, Pius XI and Pius XII—have referred to it in their Encyclicals, and the present Pope, John XXIII, mentioned it with even greater force and clarity in his coronation sermon, calling it "the first, if not indeed the only, care of the Roman Pontiff". This apostolic office is entrusted by the pope to any given Institute by delegation of divine power. Such delegation has a double purpose: the preaching of the Gospel as the prologue to the establishment of a local Church, which is possible when the teaching has been spread abroad sufficiently widely both in extent and depth. When the Church

has been firmly established—especially by the formation of a
native hierarchy—this local Church becomes the point of
departure for new missions.

In this primary task the pope is helped by a specialized
"ministry", the Sacred Congregation for the Propagation of
the Faith (*Sacra Congregatio de Propaganda Fide*), often
called merely "Propaganda". It was founded by Gregory XV
in 1622, when, conscious of papal duty with regard to the
missions, he decided to centralize the evangelization of the
whole non-Christian world in the hands of the papacy. Hence,
we might define a mission country as one in which Propaganda has established a mission. There are in fact mission
countries where the missions are not dependent on Propaganda. The countries of the Near East and Central Europe,
for example, are linked with the Sacred Congregation for
the Eastern Church because there are within their boundaries
ancient Catholic communities of the Eastern Rite (Greco-
Melchites, Byzantines, Chaldeans, Maronites, Copts, Syrians,
Armenians, etc.); Portuguese overseas possessions are linked
(as a result of Portugal's ancient privilege of the *patronato*) to
the Patriarchate of Lisbon, and come under the Consistorial
Congregation, as do the countries where Christianity has been
long established.

Thus when we speak of France as a mission country we do
not mean it in our sense of the word here. The countries
quoted and studied in this present book will be those falling
into the category established above—that is, those governed
by Propaganda.

Defined in this way, the mission countries are as follows:
the whole of Africa, with the exception of Algeria, Tunisia,
and the Portuguese possessions (subject to the Consistorial
Congregation), Egypt, Eritrea and North Ethiopia (subject
to the Congregation for the Eastern Church); all Asia, except
the Philippines, Goa and the Portuguese possessions (the

Consistorial Congregation), the Near East and Afghanistan (Congregation for the Eastern Church); all Oceania, including Australia, but excluding the Hawaiian Islands (part of the United States of America and hence under the Consistorial Congregation); in America, the West Indies, Alaska, the vicariates and prefectures apostolic of northern Canada and certain parts of Central America, Colombia, Chile, Ecuador, Paraguay, Peru and Venezuela; and in Europe, the Scandinavian countries, and parts of Albania and Jugoslavia.

What course does the development of a missionary country follow between the moment when the first missionaries arrive within its boundaries and the time comes when it is considered sufficiently firmly established for a normal hierarchy to be set up there? What is meant by vicariates and prefectures apostolic?

When a mission is sent into a pagan country it is led by a superior named by the pope: if the mission is not attached to any already existing missionary district it is given its own statute as a mission *sui juris*. When evangelization has begun to bear definite fruits and the promise of a more abundant harvest has proved not to be vain, the mission is raised to the status of a prefecture apostolic; then, as the number of Christians grows, the prefecture becomes a vicariate apostolic, and its head receives episcopal consecration, if he has not already been given it. Finally, when a missionary territory has given sufficient proof of its vitality, the pope can establish the traditional hierarchy there, dividing the country into archbishoprics and bishoprics leaving perhaps some parts of the territory, where evangelization has proceeded more slowly, with the rank of prefectures apostolic. For example, when in 1955 Pius XII established the hierarchy in French Africa, Guinea, which had been made a prefecture apostolic in 1897, consisted of a vicariate apostolic (Conakry) and two prefectures (Kankan and Zerekore); Conakry was made an archbishopric but the status of the two prefectures remained unchanged. The establishment of the hierarchy in a mission country does not mean that the country ceases to be under the control of Propaganda, but presupposes not only that the Gospel has taken firm root there, but also that the local Church already has all the marks of a Church capable of functioning normally, with fully organized centres of worship; seminaries; spiritual, social and welfare societies; Catholic Action, etc. The training of native priests, monks and nuns must be following the normal pattern. The crowning of missionary work will be the nomination of native bishops who will finally replace the "foreign" episcopate.

But if the vicar apostolic receives episcopal consecration, in what way is he different from a bishop? By the power of jurisdiction. A bishop has jurisdiction over the Church of which he is the head: this is why his jurisdiction is called ordinary jurisdiction, and why the bishop is often called the Ordinary of the district under his jurisdiction; he bears the title of his see city. The vicar apostolic is given only vicarial jurisdiction; he exercises his jurisdiction as the representative of the pope, the real bishop of the place. The pope could, if need arose, move him, instructing him to penetrate further into the territory—or even, if necessary, withdraw, just as a commander-in-chief may move his officers about or order them to manoeuvre during a campaign. Because the vicar apostolic has no church of his own he does not bear the title of the see he administers, but that of some ancient diocese that has now disappeared: he is a titular bishop, for he has only the title and not the see—the see no longer exists.

When the Catholic Church is sufficiently strongly represented in a mission country of some importance in the world at large, the pope may establish diplomatic relations with it. Such relations are not established in such countries (as they are in countries that have long been Catholic) through the medium of nuncios, but through apostolic delegates or, on a higher level, of internuncios. Thus in India an apostolic delegate was nominated in 1884, and an internuncio replaced him in 1948. In the same way, apostolic delegates were named for Japan in 1919, for South Africa in 1920, for China in 1922 (an internuncio was nominated in 1946), for Indonesia in 1947 (replaced by an internuncio in 1950), etc. An important missionary country still subject to colonial guardianship may also be given an apostolic delegate if special problems arise for the missions in their relationship with the colonial administration: thus an apostolic delegate was nominated in 1930 for what was then the Belgian Congo and Ruanda Urundi, and another was nominated in the same year for all the British possessions in Africa, and a third in 1948 for French Africa. Besides his diplomatic duties, an apostolic delegate is charged with the oversight of local Churches, and with keeping the pope informed.

The greatest advance for a missionary Church is shown, as we have said, by the nomination of native bishops enjoying the same powers, rights and prerogatives as "European" bishops. Referring back to the teaching and example of his predecessor, Pius XII declared in Encyclical *Summi Pontificatus* (October 20th, 1939) that "those who enter the Church, whatever may be their origin or their language, should know that they have an equal right of sonship in the house of the Lord, where the law and peace of Christ reign. It is in conformity with these laws of equality that the Church devotes all its care to training a native clergy up to the loftiness of its task, and so gradually augments the number of indigenous bishops." Then the pope announced the appointment of twelve bishops "representatives of races or groups of races of the most diverse kinds". Among them were the first African and first Madagascan bishops.

In 1923 Pius XI had established the first native diocese in India, and six months later, the first native diocese in China. But it was not until February 28th, 1926—the day of the promulgation of the Encyclical *Rerum Ecclesiae*—that he consecrated the first six Chinese bishops, the first fruits of the astonishing harvest of native prelates. Today they number 136. On October 30th, 1927, the first Japanese bishop received episcopal consecration from the hands of the pope himself. Then followed the first Vietnamese bishops (June 11th, 1933), the first African and Madagascan (December 29th, 1939), and the first Javanese (January 25th, 1940). In 1946 the native Church broke through another barrier with the entry into the College of Cardinals of Mgr Thomas Tien, the first Chinese cardinal. The first Indian cardinal—Mgr Gracias of Bombay—was nominated on January 12th, 1953, and the first black cardinal—Mgr Rugambwa of Rutabo (Tanganyika)—on March 28th, 1960, together with the first Japanese cardinal. During the same period the hierarchy was established in China (April 11th, 1946), in British West Africa (April 18th, 1950), Pakistan (July 15th, 1950), South Africa (January 11th, 1951), British East Africa (March 25th, 1953), French Africa (November 4th, 1955), Japan and most recently in the Belgian Congo and Ruanda Urundi (November 10th, 1959). Meanwhile new peoples saw their own priests raised to the episcopate in Korea and Basutoland.

The wonderful development in the missionary Churches in the last forty years has shown itself in a remarkable way in the increase in the number of ecclesiastical districts which have become subject to Propaganda in that time: in 1922, they numbered 315; 1939, 526; on June 30th, 1946, 556; on June 30th, 1951, 605; on June 30th, 1956, 683, and on January 1st, 1959, 702. Of these districts 166 are at present in Communist countries and together make up the "Church of Silence".

CHAPTER III

THE ORGANIZATION AND ACTIVITIES OF THE MISSIONS

Imagine a missionary, one of the many, arriving at the mission to which he has been nominated. He brings with him all his load of instructions and his linguistic, theological, scientific and practical training. He is young, full of enthusiasm and charity. What will he find on his arrival among "his" Negroes or "his" Papuans? One of two things: either he will find a mission already in being and full of life; or he will find nothing, and will have to build up everything himself, and he will thank God if he has a companion or two to help him. In any case, as soon as he arrives, he will have to preach the teaching of Jesus and bear concrete witness to his charity. To do so requires of him much self-denial, renunciation and effort. But how great will be his joy when he begins to see results—however small they may be!

On entering his mission territory, God's envoy has already cut himself off from his native country: so says *Maximum illud*: "Remember that you are not to propagate the kingdom of men, but that of Christ; that you are not to enrol citizens into any country of this world, but that of the next." In his Letter *Ab ipsis,* Pius XI confirmed Benedict XV's teaching, giving it even greater emphasis: "The Church has tried continually, in a general way with all its ministers, but very energetically with its missionaries, to turn them from any partiality for their own native land."

Pius XII found the right word when he spoke of the "supranationality" of the Church. This is an idea that the missionary must never forget. Furthermore, just as he must separate himself entirely from the interests of his native country, so too he should be totally detached from his own: he works neither for his country, nor for himself, but for the good of the people entrusted to him, and for the greater glory of God, and of God alone. The glory of his Congregation or Institute should not enter into the reckoning.

This is why his missionary training has been so stringent, and why, even before his departure for the mission, he was so thoroughly taught the language, the customs and even the diseases of his flock. "The romance of the apostolate is no longer enough", Pius XII declared. The missionary, who at his very first contact may encounter the élite among the natives, must exercise the maximum psychological insight; thus "adaptation", an ancient practice of the Church, which makes herself Greek to the Greeks and Papuan to the Papuans, is not camouflage, a trick, a disguise. It is a necessity if the Church is to succeed in showing her maternal nature to native peoples. To succeed in doing this she must show respect for native civilizations, by retaining everything in them that can be retained, and, as far as is possible, christianizing it.

To win the hearts of his flock, the missionary must not forget the excellent precepts of Pius XI: to care for the sick and make himself the friend of children; to be able to be content with a humble chapel, but as soon as possible to establish at least a dispensary if not a hospital, so doing as Christ ordered his apostles to do: "When you enter a city . . . heal those who are sick there; and tell them, the Kingdom of God is close upon you" (Luke 10. 8–9). Pius XI's advice has been widely followed, as can be seen from the fact that in 1949 there were in all the missions taken together 1,115 hospitals, as against only 600 in 1923.

It hardly needs emphasizing that it is no less important to foster education: the fight against illiteracy has been the first task undertaken in the re-christianizing of certain countries of South America. It is the first task to be undertaken if the missionary would train helpers capable of giving him effective support in the propagation of the Gospel. It is the first task to be performed if his yearning is to ameliorate the lives of the people given into his charge. Figures published in 1949 list more than three million children being taught in missionary primary schools. At the same time there were more than six hundred thousand in the secondary schools and more than three hundred thousand following courses in higher education. Certain countries were characterized by remarkable totals: there were half a million pupils and students in India, and almost forty thousand in Japan (in a Christian community of a hundred and fifty thousand). With success like this, problems are bound to appear: not the least of them has been that of non-Catholic pupils, especially in connection with the syllabus of religious instruction. Yet it is impossible to imagine a Catholic school without such instruction.

Another activity not to be neglected when missionary's peoples have advanced far enough is the Press. It must not be forgotten that it has been through the missions that printing has been introduced into a large number of countries (such as, for example, Latin America, the Philippines, India, Burma, etc.). Many missions now have their own weekly paper or their monthly or bi-monthly periodical. In Japan, a Catholic daily is published at Nagasaki and another at Tokyo. The Agency *Fides*, founded in Rome in 1927 by the Association for the Propagation of the Faith, ensures the diffusion of all news items concerning mission countries and thus is a source of news of primary importance to the missionary Press.

With these activities superimposed on the actual work of propagating the faith the responsibilities falling on the head of a mission are vast indeed.

Benedict XV defined his duties in *Maximum illud* and Pius XI delineated them more exactly in *Rerum Ecclesiae,* emphasizing the methods to be used to spread the Gospel. In the Instruction *Quum huic,* addressed by Propaganda to missionary bishops and the superiors of missionary societies, dated December 8th, 1929, the powers of the head of a mission are defined very explicitly: all the responsibility for the work of evangelization is his, and hence all the material means put at the disposal of the mission are his to administer with the help of his advisers, and hence, too, it is for him to control all missionary personnel, whether priests or helpers, lay brothers or laymen. In a word—as Benedict XV said—he should be the "soul" of his mission. This shows clearly enough the importance of his personality: a mission is a very delicate mechanism, requiring the most capable leader available at its head. As his most usual title—vicar apostolic— shows, pontifical authority is delegated totally to him.

But the qualities demanded of a simple missionary are hardly less impressive. We have already seen how great a sum of knowledge is required of him. But this would mean nothing, and with it he would be able to sow only ruins, if he were not spiritually perfect, "a model of obedience, humility, chastity and piety surpassing all others" (*Maximum illud*). His self-abnegation should be such that it is possible to see through him the one Church, impersonal and Catholic, whose mission is limited by neither space nor time.

Consider how missionary work is carried out. Three stages mark the penetration of a territory by the Gospel: making contact with local people, preaching in the proper sense of the word and the establishment of a local Church.

"In the meanwhile, let the missionaries remember that they must follow the same methods with the natives as did the divine teacher when he was on earth", Pius XI wrote in *Rerum Ecclesiae*. Put quite simply this is how the missionary should approach those to whom he desires to preach: he should beware of too much rationalism, and of all literature. Far from ignoring the local authorities, it is to them that he should go first, without forgetting the honours due to their rank. And above all, he must arm himself with a triple layer of the brass armour of patience!

Preaching itself must depend on places and circumstances: it may perhaps be better to do it by way of charitable activities. These should never be neglected. On the other hand charitable activities must never lead the missionary to forget that the spreading of the Word remains the primary act of missionary work.

What the missionary must avoid above all is using political weapons to make converts. A warning against this is to be found in the great Instruction addressed by Alexander VII to the first vicars apostolic in 1659. Special care should be taken to see that the arguments used in the course of preaching cannot be interpreted as incitements to rebellion against established authorities. The missionary has to be careful never to disturb either the local way of life or local customs. Fr de Nobili spoke out against this practice as early as the beginning of the seventeenth century. Finally, he should busy himself principally with the conversion, first of all, of the leaders of local society.

But, following the instructions of the popes, he must not be content with the successes obtained in the mission station to which God has sent him. He should not stop until the seed has been sown in the whole of the territory. Thus, if he is the head of the mission, he must distribute the heralds of the

Gospel over the whole territory and increase their numbers. If there are not enough missionary priests he should hasten the training of a local clergy that will be able to relieve them, and should train the greatest possible number of auxiliaries and catechists, and call in the help of the specialized Institutes. He should so organize his territory that no part of it is forgotten and should divide it by creating sub-stations with their own chapel, whence catechists may be sent out to teach in all the villages, even the most remote. The choice of the position for each station and each branch should not be made hastily or provisionally, but with a view to permanency; sometimes a village will be more suitable for this purpose than an administrative centre of some size. There will be at first no question of putting up fine buildings: it will be better if they are of a more humble kind, and in greater number, so that missionary work may be decentralized.

Finally, the head of the mission must not forget that the aim of his apostolate is not only to bring about the birth of the Church in a pagan land, but the establishment of a local Church that may attain its majority as soon as possible. According to the Letter *Lo sviluppo* (May 23rd, 1923), it will have done so when "it can guide itself, with its own Churches, its own clergy native to the place, and by its own methods: in a word, when it depends only on itself". But first he must remember the need to teach children in Christian schools, so giving their lives a positive orientation towards God. The success of these schools will, moreover, attract numerous non-Christian pupils, and may have an influence over them of a kind the missionary has sought in vain to obtain by other means. At this point, however, we must not forget the dangers that may arise when the majority of the pupils in a school are not Christians (as has happened fairly frequently, especially in India). We shall not enumerate again those dangers we have already pointed out—the problems posed by religious instruction, and the risk of the contamination of young Christians by subversive ideas, etc. When pupils from the upper classes have been noticed attending schools it is desirable that they should be guided towards the minor seminary, so that future priests may be looked for among them. This is why it is necessary to establish such foundations in every district as early as possible. Major seminaries, fewer in number, but no less indispensable, can be common to several regions, for there will be many losses and only very gifted souls will be able to break so completely with the way of life and customs of their forefathers. The crowning of all this work will be the raising of a native priest to the episcopate. Then the local Church will clearly have reached its majority, and if it is strong enough, the mission will be able to disappear: it will have performed its rôle to the end.

While awaiting the attainment of their high destiny, the native clergy will be a valuable support to "European" missionaries. It is not necessary to prove that their support is needed: their training has been the Church's tradition since apostolic times; it has been the primary aim of missionary endeavour since the most ancient times (in the fourteenth century the Franciscan John of Monte Corvino, the first archbishop of Pekin, was already doing it; in 1519, Leo X consecrated the first Congolese bishop; the Instruction of 1659 commends it strongly to the first vicars apostolic). The most modern characteristic of the new native clergy is its complete equality of rank, which was solemnly proclaimed in 1924 by the suppression of the privilege of precedence for apostolic missionaries. Thus, as he is called to be the equal of the European priest, the education of the native priest requires especial care: it should be identical with what seminarians receive in the countries which have long been Catholic, for we must never forget the warnings in the astonishingly prophetic instructions of Pius XI on the need for native priests to be able to relieve foreign missionaries if, when the mission country reaches independence, events compel the foreigners to withdraw. This is perhaps why the most note-worthy missionary activity in the last forty years has been the increase in the number of overseas seminaries: the Sul-picians have made themselves the masters in this field, princi-pally on the initiative of their superior Fr (later Cardinal) Verdier, for they have founded several including Hanoi (1929), Fukuoka (Japan, 1933), Kun-Ming (Yunnan, 1934) and Uidah (Dahomey: where the minor seminary was estab-lished in 1931). The students from these major seminaries are sent on to complete their studies in Europe, chiefly at the Propaganda College in Rome. At the beginning of 1954 this well-known institution had 237 students from forty different countries.

But the training of a native clergy takes many years—and the missionary needs effective help during this period. For it, he has to turn to the laity, and must train catechists. Their rôle and field of action were defined remarkably clearly by Pius XII in the discourse he gave at the second World Congress on the Apostolate of the Laity (October 5th, 1957):

> The catechist represents perhaps the most classic case of the lay apostolate both by the very nature of his profession and because he makes good the shortage of priests. It is estimated among African missionaries at least that a missionary accom-panied by six catechists does more than seven missionaries; for the catechist works in a familiar milieu, where he knows both the language and the customs; he can make contact with individuals much more easily than a missionary who has come from far away.

The catechist's function is threefold: he must contribute to the propagation of the faith, help in the teaching of religion and act as a guide to the nascent community.

Catechists perform their primary task where, the com-munity having come into being, the missionary needs an assistant to maintain it in life while he himself goes on yet further. Choosing and training them requires the greatest care—although it should not be forgotten that they are only temporary helpers, and do not make it unnecessary to train native priests. The diocese of Kudugu in the Volta Republic affords a remarkable example: its area is more than 11,500 square miles (the area of Belgium), and there are twenty-five African and missionary priests, nineteen nuns and four lay brothers for a population of 550,000 of whom 20,000 are Christians. Catechists coming from a rural background share the labours of their neighbours, while guaranteeing the direction that will be taken by the Christian community; they perform baptisms in cases of necessity, preside at Sunday prayers when the priest, at too great a distance, is unable to come and say Mass (sometimes a village is more than forty miles from the mission station and the priest can only come once a month) and say the prayers at funerals. None of this prevents them from making contact with other, still pagan, villages and making Christ known there by their words and the example of their charity. The training of these catechists is done during the dry season (which lasts seven or eight months) at a specialist school founded by Mgr Bretault at Imansgho. It lasts over four years.

But the catechist should not be the only kind of layman called to a missionary ministry, for it is in fact the duty of the whole Christian community to work at the spreading of the divine Word. It is the duty of every Christian to teach the Gospel in private: equally he should on occasion preach it in public, in the fulfilment of a collective or personal duty (as do the militant members of Catholic Action, for example). Finally, because they have been given a mandate, lay people should teach publicly—professionally, as it were. The lay mission is not, then, a state of life, but is in fact a kind of apostolate. The first concrete expressions of the fact that it had begun to be looked at in this way are scattered throughout Europe in the form of organizations: such as the *Auxiliaires*

Laïques des Missions in Belgium, *Ad Lucem* in France and the Italian Society of Medical Missionaries. Other similar societies have come into being in France, Canada, Holland and the United States of America.

Moreover, the activities of lay people should not be merely missionary: they should also (and essentially) be social and sometimes even political. They should extend into every field, including sport and culture. Their essential purpose should be the training of an active native laity. One of the oldest and most active societies of this lay missionary work is *Ad Lucem*. It was founded in 1932 at Lille under the direction of Cardinal Liénart. Its aim is to bear witness to the Gospel and participate in missionary work, everyone doing what he can in the field of his own profession.

But it is not enough for the missionary laity to establish welfare, public health and social works any more than it is for the missionary priest to create a native Church. Of necessity there must be brought into being a native laity capable of assuming its own responsibilities. The training of a native laity should therefore be orientated in the first place towards the social progress of lay people within the life of the Church. Any such activity will often encounter a great many difficulties (lack of brotherly cooperation, absence of professional conscience and standards, unfavourable conditions of work, bad feeding, health and hygiene, discouragement and loneliness, especially among the urban proletariat and, in the bush, native customs and materialism). This activity should be carried on principally among young people. It would appear that family societies are more difficult to transplant, especially into Africa. Trade union activities should not be neglected, if only to save people from the insidious infiltration of Marxist propaganda. European Christians whose aim it is to help in the training of a native laity should do so in a spirit wholly charitable and wholly disinterested, thrusting aside any remnant of colonial paternalism.

Popes since Benedict XV have abundantly proved their solicitude for the missions. On June 24th, 1944, Pius XII reminded the meeting of the Higher Councils of the Pontifical Missionary Societies of the immensely important rôle played by his predecessor: under his pontificate, 221 new districts had been created; the number of missionaries had more than doubled; the number of native clergy had increased in almost the same proportion; the number of children attending mission schools had tripled. The work of Pius XII himself was in no way less glorious, for in 1939 the number of ecclesiastical districts dependent on Propaganda was 526; at his death it had increased to 700, including the 166 that to his sorrow he had seen pass under the Communist yoke. In 1889, the year of the foundation of the Society of St Peter the Apostle (devoted to the promotion of native clergy) there were 870 priests and 2,700 seminarians natives of missionary countries. In 1939, these totals had increased eightfold and by 1959, fifteenfold. In 1939, seventy districts were entrusted to native bishops; by 1959 this total had increased to ninety-six, without taking into account auxiliary bishops.

But the popes did not confine themselves to increasing the number of missionary centres. They also took steps to ease the labours of the Lord's workers and enable the natives to adopt the Christian religion with less difficulty by ensuring that in doing so they need not lose contact with their own world. On May 2nd, 1941, Pius XII authorized the use of vernacular Rituals in New Guinea, China, Japan, Indo-China and India. On August 8th, 1942, this privilege was extended to all the African missions. In 1948, it was the turn of the missions of Indonesia and Oceania to be given the same privilege. But translation difficulties considerably delayed the publication of these Rituals. The first Latin-Hindustani Ritual was not published until 1950, and then only for the nine dioceses of North India. The Latin-Malagasy Ritual appeared in 1953, and the Latin-Japanese in 1957.

More important was the authorization given by Pius XII, and dated March 10th, 1949, for the celebration of the Mass in the literary language of China (except in the Canton area). A similar privilege had been granted in 1615 by Paul V, but had never been exercised. Since 1955, other more restricted privileges have been granted to certain countries: the right to sing the *Kyrie, Gloria, Credo* and other chants of the Ordinary or the Mass in the common language of certain dioceses of Indonesia, Formosa, India and Africa; the reading of scriptural texts in the native language after they have been read in Latin was granted to the diocese of Fort Jameson in Northern Rhodesia in 1954; the transfer of Rogation processions to the actual time of sowing in Madagascar in 1957.

Several pontifical Instructions have given strong encouragement to the development of native religious music, in particular the Encyclical *Musicae Sacrae Disciplina* (December 25th, 1955), in which we read these words of great wisdom:

> Many of the peoples entrusted to the ministry of missionaries greatly enjoy musical rhythms, and use singing in ceremonies dedicated to the worship of idols. It is not good for the heralds of Christ to underestimate or wholly neglect this effective aid to their apostolate. Hence the messengers of the Gospel in pagan lands should willingly devote themselves in their apostolic ministry to the fostering of this love of religious music which is so strong among the people given into their charge. In this way, these peoples will come to prefer to their own religious songs—which often excite the admiration of the most civilized foreigners—similar Christian canticles which extol in their own tongue, and with their own traditional melodies, the truths of the faith, the life of our Lord, and the praises of our Lady and the saints.

This is the modern form of the christianization of pagan rites, foreshadowed by St Gregory the Great as early as the end of the sixth century. Nevertheless, missionaries must take care to introduce the Gregorian Chant into pagan countries as recommended by the Instruction *De Sacra Musica et Sacra Liturgia* promulgated on September 3rd, 1958, by the S. Congregation of Rites:

> Where there are peoples who rejoice in their own musical culture, missionaries will also endeavour to use native music in worship, with due precautions. They should in particular devote themselves to so arranging the exercises of devotion that the native faithful can also express their religious sentiments in their own language and in melodies suitable for their country. But it should not be forgotten that Gregorian melodies can, as is widely recognized, frequently be equally easily sung by natives, for they often have a measure of affinity with their own melodies.

All these concessions prove the manifest anxiety of Pius XII to demonstrate the catholicity of the Church. In the course of the International Liturgical Congress held at Assisi in September, 1956, however, the missionary bishops asked for more freedom in the use of native languages in divine worship, for a new translation of the rites of the Mass and Baptism stressing the more important sections (and especially asking for the functional restoration of the Mass of the catechumens) and lastly for a more fluid uniformity, so that missionaries might make adaptations (in, for example, the simplification of pontifical vestments for use in hot countries).

Papal solicitude has also been manifested with regard to sacred art in missionary countries. Native Christian art should have a twofold concern: to provide as inspiration for the Church's prayer whatever seems most beautiful to the natives; and to be a source of prestige and glory for the Church. Above all, it should never be forgotten that before pleasing us, native religious art should please natives: hence it is preferable to leave European representations of Christ and our Lady in Chinese churches if the Chinese think that Chinese Christs and Madonnas are not "true". In many countries, however, very encouraging results have been obtained (this is especially true of the Congo), and sometimes, as in India, there has appeared an idealist art, a hybrid of traditional and Western art. As Mgr Costantini (organizer of the 1940 exhibition of Christian missionary art at the Vatican) said: "The Christian idea must not serve art: art should serve the Christian idea; this idea is not patient of modification, but at whatever cost the means of expression must be adapted to the thought to be expressed."

Most bewildering of the problems facing the head of a mission is that of means, especially of financial means. Natives can contribute only in a very small measure to these needs, and help must therefore come from outside—or, in other words, from Propaganda. But the means available are very small compared with the tasks to be performed: the sums received yearly by the pontifical missionary societies do not exceed twenty million dollars—an amount insufficient to build a modern university on the American scale, and Catholic universities are needed in highly civilized countries such as India, Vietnam and Japan.

Despite the precarious state of finances, the material situation has improved greatly at many mission stations, especially since the end of the last war. The period of missionary romanticism, when foundations depended on good fortune, has given way to a better: buildings, schools, churches, mission houses are all built solidly and built to last. Means of communication have improved; scientific methods are now used in the propagation of the faith itself; the radio is regularly employed for this purpose in South America. But seeing the vastness of the task remaining to be done how can any Christian not feel guilty of neglecting to lend his help by participating actively in one of the great pontifical aid societies? The first of them—the Missionary Union of the Clergy—was founded in 1916, and became a pontifical society in 1924. Its aim is to bring to an end indifference about the missions in Christian countries. In 1950 the Union had 217,000 priest members throughout the world. There are three big societies for lay people: the Association for the Propagation of the Faith, which requires full participation, not merely philanthropic gestures, from the faithful (it asks for continual prayer for the 30,000 missionary priests, and education with a view to awakening the consciences of Christian people about the missions); the Society of St Peter the Apostle, founded at Caen in 1889 by Jeanne Bigard, on the basis of an idea of Mgr Cousin, then vicar apostolic at Nagasaki, with the aim of helping in the recruitment and training of native clergy (it became a pontifical missionary society in 1920); and the Society of the Holy Childhood, with the object of gaining the support of Christian children through prayer, works of charity and sacrifices for all kinds of welfare work and education in mission countries (maternity homes, nurseries, orphanages, schools). In other words, its aim is more than "the buying of Chinese babies"—the aspect of this society generally represented to the public. Indeed, in mission countries, according to statistics published in 1950, there are 386,000 children in nurseries, 110,000 children in orphanages, and more than 2,800,000 children in schools. Another aim of this society is the training of the children belonging to it in Catholic Action.

Despite the glowing picture presented by the results achieved in the course of the last forty years, missions still find numerous thorny problems in their way. First among these is the proliferation of Protestant sects. These are very active—and they leave natives aghast before the multitude of Churches all laying claim to Christ, but often lacking his spirit. As long ago as 1936 there were seventy-two non-Catholic Christian churches in Japan. In India, there are about 150 non-Catholic missions, representing a total of some sixty-six sects. Then there is the propaganda of non-Christian religions: when faced with the success of Catholicism, these have sometimes found a new lease of life: this has happened with Buddhism in Burma and Thailand, Hinduism in some parts of Central and North India, and especially with Islam, in the whole of Black Africa, whether it be orthodox Islamism, such as is taught by the famous El Azhar university of Cairo or the Islamism of dissident sects, such as the Aga Khan's Ismailis, who are very strongly entrenched in Zanzibar and Tanganyika. At the present time, the advance of Islam in black Africa is twice as fast as that of Christianity, because of the advantages it offers black people in, for instance, recognizing polygamy, and being able to explain its teaching and worship in half a day instead of four or five years of catechetical instruction.

	Catholicism		Islam	
	Adherents in millions	Percentage of total population	Adherents in millions	Percentage of total population
Asia . . .	13	1	227	16
Africa . . .	21	9	85	38
Oceania–Pacific Is. .	27	21	66	56
America . . .	150	55	—	—
Europe . . .	247	37	27	4
Totals . .	458	17	405	15

Between 1920 and 1950, Catholicism grew from about 390 to about 460 million baptized adherents; during the same period Islam increased its membership from 250 to 405 million.

Another obstacle to the propagation of the faith is materialism, which is all too often encouraged under the pretext of neutralism or secularism by the officials of the colonial powers. A native whose only ideal is the acquisition of material goods soon finds his hopes illusory and quickly falls prey to Communism which, after its Asian successes, is now penetrating insidiously across Africa from coast to coast, awaiting the moment when the fruit may be plucked painlessly. This is why missionary activity in the social sphere has become so important today.

THE WORK OF MISSIONS

Papal injunctions have brought into being a new activity in the missionary Church: as we have already seen, it has been given the task of training an active missionary laity. In order to do so, it has increased the number of its teaching establishments of every kind, from the school in the African bush to the Indian university college, including technical and professional schools intended to awaken in native workers a lively awareness of their professional duty. Other problems arise as the nations of Asia and Africa reach political maturity: the industrialization of these young States gives rise to a hitherto non-existent urban proletariat, ill-equipped to defend itself against wicked shepherds; malnutrition, sometimes reaching famine proportions, ravages many missions; some districts in Central Africa are being depopulated at a disturbing rate; the peasantry of North and West Africa is being rapidly proletarianized. These things must be quickly and energetically dealt with if we do not want to see the "pernicious errors" referred to by Pius XII drown what the missionary Church has done. This is why it is necessary to increase even further the number of schools, enlarge the work for public health, make philanthropic work a subject for constant concern and ensure that Christian social work takes firm root in mission territories.

It is not our intention to refer again in detail to the subject of education, but it requires to be mentioned that the successful results of mission schools sometimes lead to the Catholics in these schools being in a large minority: in India, Catholics account for only 25 per cent of boys and 29 per cent of girls, while 66 per cent of the boys and 54 per cent of the girls are not even Christian. In Japan, where in 1949 the Christian community numbered only 150,000, 370,000 children, of whom 27,000 were girls, were being sent to Catholic schools of all grades.

Medical work

This is perhaps the best-known form of missionary work. The missionary sisters who devote themselves with total self-abnegation to lepers are familiar to many of us. But is it widely known that some congregations of nuns study at Catholic or State universities for medical and surgical diplomas, with the sole intention of using them in mission countries, at hospitals and maternity homes in the bush? There is certainly a great deal to be done in this field in mission countries for there are countless diseases to be fought. In a set of figures relating to sixty-nine mission areas scattered around the world in Africa, Asia, Oceania and South America, leprosy is mentioned forty-eight times, malaria twenty-eight, tuberculosis twenty-six, venereal diseases twenty, epidemic diseases (especially small-pox, measles and influenza) twelve, intestinal diseases (dysentery, etc.) and sleeping sickness ten times each; skin diseases and parasitic diseases nine times each.

It is indeed a sad list. Every missionary area has its dispensary. In many of them, there are one or two or even more hospitals in every district. Cardinal Rugambwa has five at present under construction in his diocese of Rutabo in Tanganyika. A sanatorium is being built in the Seychelles Islands. Sometimes missionary medical work is damaged by lack of understanding on the part of governments: in 1958 the dispensaries of the Sudan Mission (in what had been the Condominion) were forced to close their doors by order of the authorities. But the strongest brake on activity in this field is the shortage of physicians: although there is one doctor for every 700 inhabitants of the United States, and one for every 950 inhabitants of Europe, there is only one for 2,500 inhabitants in South America, one for 8,200 in India, one for 25,000 in French Africa, one for 36,000 in Pakistan, one for 60,000 in Vietnam and one for 90,000 in Cambodia. In mission countries the need for doctors is tragic; and societies of lay missionaries, such as *Ad Lucem*, are not well enough supported.

We have seen that the most widespread disease is still leprosy. It is a disease which is not very infectious, but is terrifying in its mutilating effects. According to Raoul Follereau, who has devoted himself unwearyingly to the moral and social rehabilitation of the unfortunate people infected with it, there are from ten to twelve million lepers in the world—one in every two hundred of the world's inhabitants, one for every two cases of tuberculosis. In 1952 there were ninety-seven leper colonies totally dependent on the missions, caring for 26,437 cases. In addition in the same year nuns were working among lepers in 122 State foundations with 46,587 cases.

In all, no less than 128 missionary institutes devote themselves to these unfortunate people. For a long time, unable to prevent this disease, doctors had to be content with stabilizing it by the use of therapeutics, sometimes violent in action, based principally on oil of chaulmoogra. Then came the discovery of sulphonamides, making it possible to stop the advance of the disease and cicatrize the ulcers, so that it has become possible to regard many lepers as healed and beyond danger of relapse, and to return them to everyday life. There is now great hope that we shall see the total disappearance of this disease: in 1952 a Marian Sister, Sister Marie-Suzanne, succeeded in isolating the causative organism of leprosy, *Mycobacterium marianum.* Starting from this bacillus she has prepared a vaccine, which is still in the experimental stage.

A short summary will give some idea of the extent of missionary medical work: in 1923, there were in all the territories under Propaganda 589 mission hospitals and 1,800 dispensaries; in 1949 there were 1,079 hospitals and 3,130 dispensaries. In the same period the number of hospitals in Oceania increased from fifteen to 136, in China from 100 to 216, and in the Belgian Congo from sixty-seven to 196. It must be added that in 1957 the leper colony on Wallis Island in French Polynesia was closed as the patients there were considered healed. The high concentration of hospitals in some districts of Africa has made it possible to obtain very good results there.

Medical help is usefully complemented by social help. There are orphanages, nurseries and homes for the aged in which numerous missionary and native sisters spend themselves without counting the cost. These sisters are indeed the missions' maids of all work. Between 1935 and 1950 the number of nuns working in the missions rose from 50,000 (with 18,000 natives) to 61,000 (of whom 38,000 were natives).

Philanthropic work

Among the obstacles to missionary work we have emphasized Communism and said how perilous its effects can be among young peoples still only in the earliest stage of material progress. The humanitarian work of the missions is directed against things favourable to the growth of subversive ideas: slavery in all its forms (even the most modern), malnutrition, alcoholism, exacerbated nationalism (which very often expresses itself in xenophobia or racism seized on and exploited infallibly by evil shepherds for their own benefit).

Surprising as it may seem, slavery still exists today, notably in Arabia. What can only be called slave-ships make frequent raids on African territories, achieving success among Moslems by promising them they will make the pilgrimage to Mecca, and taking them to Arabia where they are sold like cattle. In 1945 UNESCO published a detailed report on this matter. Apart from this case of this scandalous trade, slavery no longer exists except in more or less disguised forms, such as, for example, the child labour forced on families in debt to money-lenders (reported from the prefecture apostolic of 'N'Zerekore in Guinea). A kind of feudal servitude exists in Urundi (reported from the vicariate apostolic of Kitega). In Burma, some still semi-savage races practise female slavery. In some parts of Madagascar and the Sahara, although it is no longer legal, slavery still persists in people's mental outlook: to the Moslem, a Negro is always a slave. The most common form of semi-slavery is feudal family servitude, still alive over a large part of Black Africa, although it is tending to disappear as a result of the activities of advanced Africans. The custom of dowries, whereby women are demeaned, is being strongly combated by all heads of missions, and particularly by native bishops, with the help of female lay missionaries and, of course, of nuns. Work has been started in the fight against child marriage, polygamy (where Christian families are fighting alongside advanced non-Christians for monogamous marriage), against the compulsory remarriage of widows to one of the heirs of the dead man. The aim is to make the African woman free. When she becomes a Christian, she often takes her part in the struggle, either in one of the societies such as Catholic Action or the Legion of Mary, or by doing a job of value to society, working as an infirmarian, a midwife, a social worker or a teacher. At Duala a group of African members of Catholic Action has undertaken a vigorous campaign against prostitution. In the same field, action is being taken in Japan against clandestine buyers of daughters of poor families, who then make them prostitutes.

But the most tragic spectacle in the world today is incontestably the hunger raging around three-quarters of the globe.

Never forget that two people out of three are underfed. The inquiry mentioned above showed that out of eighty-seven mission districts, hunger was severe in fourteen, with food shortages and sometimes real famine; in forty-one others, malnutrition is the rule, although there is no famine; only thirty-two proved to be free from hunger (and among these were the missions in Sweden, Norway and certain Canadian dioceses). It is true that in some dioceses, although there are food shortages, this is partly the fault of the native, who "does not like agricultural work" (e.g. Kengi in the Congo), or whose natural indifference leads him to live from hand to mouth (e.g. Wallis-Futana, Polynesia). The first fight to be undertaken against hunger is that to arm the native with a spade and a hoe and teach him the virtues of agriculture. In many parts of Africa the problem of malnutrition is a matter not of quantity but of quality, and compels missionaries to transform themselves into teachers of dietetics and urge the need for a diet richer in proteins. Finally, we have the tragic confirmation of this truth in the replies from India which show famine conditions of the most violent kind, often accompanied by, or resulting from, natural catastrophes such as floods, irregular monsoons and crop fires. The inculcation of notions of foresight and economy among natives, the rationalization of crops and methods, and the teaching of discipline in eating are the tasks facing missionaries and their helpers in this field.

Another scourge Christians often have to fight is the alcoholism ruling in various degrees almost everywhere. Whites must certainly bear a large part of the blame for its spread, but not the whole of it. Indeed, although an advanced Congolese will declare that the fact that he has advanced makes it necessary for him to drink whisky because all white men drink whisky (as has actually happened) there are in the deepest parts of the bush natives not far removed from the primitive state who distil abominable spirits just as easily able to kill or confuse as the most refined products of civilization. And what is there to be said about native beer, brewed no one knows how, capable of bringing fire and sword to South Africa,[1] responsible, it is said, for 80 per cent of marital crimes and catastrophes in Tanganyika? Alcoholism has many possible causes—for example, the hard work demanded of the workers on tea plantations in India and of the pearl fishers of Ceylon. The most tragic is that sometimes, after putting a very heavy tax on alcohol, a local government will itself urge its consumption (reported from the vicariate apostolic of Villavicencio in Colombia). Other governments, on the contrary, have taken strong measures against alcoholics (these include certain Indian States, among them Madras). Action taken by missionaries sometimes meets with indifference or runs foul of custom. Unfortunately it seems that recent years have seen a recrudescence of alcoholism, perhaps related to the increase in wealth of some towns on the west coast of Africa. At Dakar, it has advanced so far that it has become necessary to make regulations governing the sale of fuel alcohol. This is undoubtedly a very serious social problem, about which the laity will have to think very seriously.

But the question that is holding all the attention of the missionary bishops because it is of burning importance is that of nationalism and the racialism it sometimes brings in its train.

While recognizing the right of colonial peoples to aspire to independence,[2] the Church has never stopped reminding Catholics that the religion of Christ is a religion of love and charity, embracing all men in common brotherhood, whatever their race or the colour of their skins. This being so, she

[1] It should be remembered that the most recent racial incidents there grew out of the abolition of the right to brew beer freely for their own use that had been granted the native population.

[2] For an examination of the teaching of the Church as it concerns the new national states of Asia and Africa, see Chapter V below.

urges Catholics to participate in patriotic movements, for in them they can play a moderating rôle: their influence may prevent irreparable mistakes. The African tends to see racialism directed against him everywhere. Reacting against it, he himself is tempted to act with race hatred of the blindest kind against everything that is not African the instant he wins his independence. Indeed, African racialism is not merely something between whites and negroes, but also exists, in even more virulent forms, between the various tribes living together within the same State. Recent events in the Congo have given all too obvious proof of this. This same state of mind is also to be found in some parts of Tanganyika, Gabon and Chad (where the Scout movement, recently successfully introduced among young Catholics, is waging a lively and effective war against it). In practice, segregation in fact if not in law exists in several countries: in the West Indies, between Negroes, half-castes, quadroons and other groups with different proportions of coloured blood; and in Colombia between Negroes and Indians. In Indonesia it expresses itself on the political plane, in the guise of parties exclusively intended for this or that ethnic or religious group: this was one of the reasons for the recent suppression of political parties by President Soecarno, for the government has always taken steps against racial or religious discrimination of any kind.

The Church is also fighting against a form of segregation long familiar: the Indian caste system, which has been officially abolished by the government, but nevertheless still exists in practice. "The age-old caste system in India cannot disappear in a few years, despite the Constitution", a native bishop has said. And it should be noticed that the abolition of barriers between castes, practised systematically in a certain number of Indian districts, has held back the conversion of some social classes for many years; it will be recalled that in past centuries different missions were necessary to evangelize the different classes.

We cannot pass over in silence the fact that the government of one important mission country—South Africa—has brought racial segregation into being by legal action. The Catholic Church cannot but protest in the presence of such an unhappy situation. It has had the pleasure of seeing the Anglican Church join with it in its expressions of humanity and fraternity. In contrast, the Afrikander Church (a Calvinist Church of Dutch origin) supports the policy of the government. The solution of this much debated problem in human relations is to be sought only in prudent and methodical planning and in the practice of charity and justice.

The means sanctioned by the Catholic Church for finding a solution to this grave problem are: great prudence in "regulating the progress of backward races" and with prudence "so as not to aggravate suspicions and rancour, a large measure of Christian charity" which "forbids hatred and scorn for human beings" and "forbids ill-will, resentment and mistrustful prejudices", and with these, too, justice, for justice demands recognition of rights (the counterpart of duties freely accepted) and the right to exercise them freely, because any act of discrimination is "an offence against the rights of the human being". In 1957, the policy of *apartheid* had been made official and was being systematically applied when, on July 6th, the bishops published a declaration restating the position they had adopted five years earlier and condemning the policy pursued by the government. The principle behind this policy—the preservation of "white civilization"—is intrinsically evil: "apartheid is sometimes represented as separate development, giving different races the possibility of each pursuing its own evolution in the social and cultural spheres" but in practice progress is made subordinate to the supremacy of the white race. Nevertheless, the condemnation of the principle of apartheid as something intrinsically evil does not mean that perfect equality could be established in South Africa by a mere stroke of the pen. Nothing is more obvious than the existence of profound differences between the different groups in our population, making immediate and total integration impossible. Citizens could not fully share equally in political and economic institutions, in as much as they do not share a common cultural heritage. All social changes must be brought about gradually if they are not to be disastrous.

The bishops declared that the rigours of *apartheid* have embittered those suffering under it. For them the order of the day has become "revolution not evolution". Hence the bishops issued a solemn appeal to all white people of good will, asking them to abandon the practice in their own lives: "Segregation, although officially not permitted in our churches, is nevertheless practised in many of our organizations: in our schools, seminaries, convents and hospitals, and in the social life of our faithful. In the light of Christ's teaching, this cannot be tolerated for ever."

When recent events supervened in South Africa, the Church made a fresh stand against the policy of racial segregation.[3] In Tanganyika and Northern Rhodesia the bishops have adopted an identical position regarding relations between negroes and whites.

The social question

Pius XII brought light to bear on the importance of the social problem by denouncing the spread of Communist ideas: "It is the duty of all, as far as is possible, to ameliorate, lighten and assuage the sufferings, miseries and pains of our brethren in this life. Charity can in part correct the injustices

[3] Notice that in the United States of America (not a mission country, because dependent on the Consistorial Congregation) the bishops published a joint declaration in November 1958, declaring that "segregation is irreconcilable with Christian charity".

of the social order, but it is not enough in itself: justice must first be confirmed, imposed and put into effect."

But social action and political action often go together, and social action in mission countries hastens their political evolution once a group of people has become fully aware of its responsibilities. Hence it is necessary to be very prudent when acting in this matter, and make sure that the leaders to whom the societies brought into being in this field are entrusted are mature and well trained. It is therefore necessary never to lose sight of the Christian orientation which should characterize the solutions suggested for problems; one must always begin from the concrete if one is to reach the concrete as far as local situations are concerned. It is to give help in the carrying out of this task that social secretariats have been created since 1948 in many towns in black Africa (Duala, Bangui, Brazzaville, Lome, Conakry, Bamako, Dakar, etc.) as well as at Dalat in Vietnam. The participation of natives is important (in Vietnam only natives can be used) both in the directorate and in specialized executive groups. Although brought into being within the framework of the missions, the social secretariats are completely independent from them. Their primary task is to advance the social education of natives through the use of a concrete problem as an example of method, to be jointly analysed and then given to the specialist groups for attempts to find solutions. In Togoland, the problem studied was the amelioration of the lot of women, who have often not been allowed to progress as far as the men; while for natives who have progressed there was brought into being an economic and social studies circle, given as its first subject for study Trade Unions, their rôle, aims and aspirations. At Bangui, the attention of the local circle was directed towards the amelioration of local conditions: its conclusions were accepted by the government and in 1952–3 the building of a model village gave concrete expression to the results of its research. At Duala an attack was made on the rise in the cost of living by the organization of model shops, making it possible (through the action of a circuit court that also had to be set up) to sell basic products (plantain, macabo, rice, etc.) 60 to 65 per cent cheaper than they were being sold by the ordinary shopkeeper—to the great chagrin of the Bamileke middlemen, and other dishonest traders. At Duala, the social secretariat's first task was to spread the social teaching of the Church by publishing a pamphlet setting out a comparison of the three doctrines —Marxism, capitalism and Catholicism—striving for mastery in the world. A Christian social (political) movement, and Christian trade unions came into being with independence in 1951. The Vietnamese Confederation of Christian Workers, the successor to a local branch of the Confederation of French Christian Workers, is the most important trade union organization in the country today, with a large number (actually at present a majority) of non-Christian members, as well as Christians. Through its activities Vietnam has now become socially the most advanced of the Asiatic countries, alone in having collective agreements in all fields of economic activity.

In many missions the amelioration of the lot of the workers poses many grave problems. In most places the agricultural working class is small, except perhaps in the great tea plantations of India, where a huge body of native workers, unlettered and caring little for improvement, is in peril of falling victim to any kind of propaganda. But as soon as industry appears, the native who dreams of an easy life of material comfort hesitates hardly at all before going and signing on; but reality quickly proves different from his dream: uprooted, avid for pleasure (found by him in the cinema), unable to save, the native workman very soon falls victim to discouragement and runs the risk of becoming a prey to evil leaders.

As a result, in many missions where there are large centres of population, the creation of Christian trade unions has been attempted in order to make possible for natives some amelioration of the conditions of life in the first place, and some social progress in the second. This has been done in the Congo, the Cameroons, the French African States and French West Indies.

A very special kind of social action has appeared in Japan: the social rehabilitation of rag-pickers and tramps has been undertaken at Kobe on the initiative of a French religious (Fr Vallade), and at Tokyo on the initiative of a girl from the upper classes, Maria Reiko Kitahara, "the angel of Ant Town".

Another form of social action now commanding a good deal of attention from the heads of missions is the founding of Catholic Action and youth movements. Catholic Action in various forms has appeared almost everywhere except perhaps in certain predominantly rural Indian dioceses, where no one has yet been able to find a formula corresponding to the mental outlook of the various social strata in the communities. Catholic Action is very much alive even in countries where Catholics constitute a very small minority in the population, such as Sweden and Norway. Special mention must be made of the Legion of Mary, which is very active in India, Ceylon, Burma, Borneo, Korea, Japan, Colombia and many African states (including West Africa, Ghana, Sierra Leone, Kenya, Nyasaland, the Congo, etc.). At Brazzaville, it has undertaken the training of catechists: recruiting figures for catechists have tended to drop because natives no longer find in the office the prestige it used to confer. Remember, too, that in China the Legion of Mary is the soul of Catholic resistance to the lure of "patriotism". Japan is characterized by the vitality of its Catholic Action organizations.

A last form of social action, no longer to be neglected, is that carried on through Press, radio and cinema. After a fairly long eclipse, missionary publications began, after 1945, to appear again almost everywhere in Africa and in the Asian countries that escaped Communism. Because of the very large number of parochial publications and periodicals belonging to the different religious societies it is difficult to establish reliable statistics.

Circulations are usually rather small; only a few publications in great centres of population in Africa and Japan exceed 5,000 copies; those that reach 10,000 seem to be very rare. Often a single copy is read by five or six persons, especially in Africa, where the negro who can read loves to do so, seriously and with attention. But he is too poor to buy a newspaper regularly. Undoubtedly, the rapid development of means of communication—the radio, television and the cinema—poses serious problems in mission countries not only with regard to programmes but also concerning transmitters and centres of distribution; these are out of the question because of the small resources at the disposal of the missions. It is nevertheless a problem requiring study as soon as possible.

CHAPTER IV

AROUND THE WORLD
WITH THE MISSIONS

Paying homage to the missionary work of his predecessor, Pius XII, in *Evangelii praecones*, outlined this exciting comparison between 1926 and 1951 in regard to the propagation of the faith in mission countries:

> In 1926 the number of Catholic missions amounted to 400, but today it is almost 600. At that date the number of Catholics in the missions did not exceed 15,000,000, while today it is almost 28,000,000. At that time the number of native and foreign priests in the missions was about 14,800; today their number is more than 26,800. Then all bishops in the missions were foreigners; during the past twenty-five years eighty-eight missions have been entrusted to native clergy. . . . In China and some parts of Africa the ecclesiastical hierarchy has been juridically established; three very important Plenary Councils have been held, the first in 1934 in Indochina, the second in 1937 in Australia and the third last year in India. Minor seminaries have been greatly increased and strengthened. The number of those studying in major seminaries, which twenty-five years ago was only 1,770, is now 4,300; moreover, many regional seminaries have been built.

In the period of almost ten years since then, progress has been at least as great. In 1959, the number of Catholics in mission countries had increased to 33,700,000; the number of priests to 27,150 and the number of students at major seminaries to 4,132. Moreover, to these totals must be added 10,334 brothers, 67,485 sisters, more than 110,000 catechists and almost 160,000 teachers. The number of districts entrusted to native bishops had reached ninety-six, leaving out of account the areas that had passed under the Communist yoke where, when this happened, there were forty-three districts under the direction of native prelates and almost six million faithful.

The table below shows the progress made by the Catholic religion in each of the five continents (the figures indicate the number of baptized in thousands).

	1880	1933	1949	1955
Asia .	3,180	7,000	8,970	5,723
Oceania .	670	2,150	3,030	3,968
Africa .	1,150	4,945	11,015	18,223
America.	900	2,915	4,037	5,140
Europe .	700	900	890	77
	6,600	17,910	27,942	33,131

(The Churches of Silence are not included in the figures for 1955; the decrease indicated in Europe between 1933 and 1949 is due to the fact that during this period the Balkan countries—Greece, Bulgaria, Rumania, Albania, etc.—were transferred to the S. Congregation for the Eastern Church.)

Between 1885 and 1950 the number of Catholics expressed as a percentage of the population as a whole increased from 0·4 to 1·0 in Asia; 2·7 to 9·0 in Africa; and from 15·0 to 18·0 in Oceania. In all the mission countries taken together it increased from 5·5 to 8·5. But differences from one country to another were very marked. In China in 1947 half of one per cent of the people were Catholics; in India and Indonesia, despite the actual number of Catholics (5,500,000 and 1,000,000 respectively), one per cent of the population were Catholic. By contrast, the proportion of Catholics reaches

13 per cent in the Cameroons, 17 per cent in Togoland, 19 per cent in Australia, 21 per cent in Madagascar, 26 per cent in Uganda, 34 per cent in the Congo, and 49 per cent in Urundi and Gabon. The figures vary widely from one area to another within these territories: for example, in Togoland the proportion exceeds 30 per cent on the coast, but is less than 10 per cent in the north of the country.

Having looked at the general figures, we can now take a rapid glance at the five continents, examining the principal countries dependent on Propaganda.

EUROPE

The European countries under the control of Propaganda are Gibraltar, Scandinavia (Denmark, Finland, Iceland, Norway, Sweden), northern Albania, and part of Jugoslavia (these two last are now under Communist domination). Gibraltar is a diocese, while in Scandinavia there are four dioceses (*Copenhagen*, Stockholm, Oslo and Trondheim) and three vicariates apostolic (Northern Norway, Finland and *Iceland*).[1]

Denmark

Denmark was closed to Catholicism after the reformation: any missionary attempting to enter the country ran the risk of a death sentence. Freedom of worship was restored in 1849; three missionaries had already arrived by 1850; by 1890 there were 200 and by 1937, 900. The country was made a prefecture apostolic in 1868, then a vicariate in 1892, and finally a diocese in 1953. Greenland is linked with it. There are 27,000 Catholics in a population of four millions and a half.

---

[1] The dioceses and districts above printed in *italics* are entrusted to native prelates.

Sweden

Although closed like Denmark, Sweden was nevertheless made a vicariate as early as 1783. It became a diocese in 1953. The country has 26,000 Catholics in a population of 7,400,000 inhabitants of various nationalities. There are sixty-one priests in the diocese, of whom twenty-seven are seculars; among them there are eight Swedes—six of them seculars—all converts. The bishop is Mgr Nelson, a Danish Benedictine.

Norway

Norway was at first dependent on the vicariate apostolic of Sweden, but became a prefecture in 1869. Divided into three districts in 1933, it then comprised the vicariate apostolic of Oslo (made a diocese in 1953), the mission *sui juris* of Central Norway (made a prefecture apostolic in 1914, a vicariate apostolic in 1953 and quite recently raised to diocesan status as the diocese of Trondheim) and the mission *sui juris* of Northern Norway, made a prefecture in 1944 and then, quite recently, a vicariate. The bishop of Oslo is a member of the Society of Mary; the diocese of Trondheim is entrusted to the Picpus Fathers, and the vicariate of Northern Norway to the Society of the Holy Family, which maintains four stations north of the Arctic Circle, between the sixty-ninth and seventy-first parallels. There are seven priests for a district a third of the size of France with a population of 360,000—20,000 of them Laplanders, among whom there are 250 Catholics. In the whole of Norway there are 5,000 Catholics in a population of three million and a half.

Finland

Finland has 2,200 Catholics in a population of four millions. It is a vicariate apostolic constituted in 1920 and entrusted to the Dutch Province of the Fathers of the Sacred

Heart of Saint Quentin. In 1945, a party of French Dominicans started a Catholic circle at Helsinki.

Iceland

Iceland, detached from the vicariate of Denmark in 1923
and made a prefecture, then raised to a vicariate in 1929, is
entrusted to the Montfort Fathers; the vicar apostolic is a
native of the country and bears the ancient local title of
Holar. There are about 600 Catholics in a population of
147,000.

Gibraltar

The see of Gibraltar was created in 1910. The bishop, Mgr
Fitzgerald, is Irish; he is assisted by eleven secular priests.
With a population of 25,000, this British possession has
22,000 Catholics.

AMERICA

The territories on the American continent subject to Propaganda form three distinct groups: the Canadian Far North,
the West Indies and certain parts of South America.

The missions of the Far North

These missions are to be found in the lands of the Canadian
North-west Territory, Labrador, around Hudson Bay and
among the islands of the Arctic Ocean wherever there are
inhabitants. The earliest missions date from 1845, when the
huge vicariate of the North-west was created to evangelize
the Indians. Today this territory is made up of five provinces
with fifteen dioceses and eight vicariates. Only the vicariates
still depend on Propaganda: five of them are in Indian
country and three in Eskimo; all are entrusted to the Oblates
of Mary Immaculate. In the 900,000 square miles of the five
"Indian" vicariates there are still 140,000 unconverted
Indians. The three Eskimo vicariates stretch for 1,500,000

square miles and have a population of about 10,000 continually migrating Eskimos. The first missions in this region met
with tragedy with the martyrdom in 1912 of Frs Rouvière
and Leroux. The first baptisms were administered in 1917
despite the continuing hatred of witch doctors, who still have
a great deal of power over the primitive tribes. But some of
them have been converted and the daughter of one of them
made her profession among the Grey Sisters of Montreal in
February 1951: she was the first Eskimo nun. After forty-
three years of missionary work, 20 per cent of the Eskimos
are now Catholics: 1,200 out of the 6,000 living in the
vicariate apostolic of Hudson Bay, 300 out of 1,200 in the
vicariate of Mackenzie and about a hundred out of the 2,000
in that of Labrador, founded as recently as 1945. There are
about sixty missionaries, helped by fifteen brothers and
twenty of Montreal's Grey Sisters, working in the hospitals
and boarding schools at Aklavik and Chesterfield. In 1948
a missionary station was established at the Magnetic Pole.

The West Indies and Central America

Propaganda administers seventeen missionary districts in
this region: an archdiocese, nine dioceses, six vicariates and
a prefecture. The archdiocese is that of Port of Spain (Trini-
dad) and the prefecture Tarahumara (Mexico). Both French
West Indian islands, Guadeloupe and Martinique, are dioceses. Both have the same problems—under-employment,
malnutrition, alcoholism, Communistic influences and moral
laxity (but the number of irregular unions and illegitimate
children is decreasing rapidly). The newest diocese is that
of Nassau (Bahamas), created on July 5th, 1960, to replace
the vicariate of the Bahamas: the new diocese has 16,600
Catholics in a total population of 55,000; there are thirty-two
priests (four of them seculars and twenty-one Benedictines),
and sixty-two nuns, twenty-four of them members of a local
congregation. Scattered through the islands of the archipelago

there are nineteen parishes and thirty-six lesser missionary stations. The mission has opened twenty-three elementary schools (attended by 3,670 pupils) and five secondary schools. The bishop, Mgr Hagerty, is an American Benedictine. Nine young native men are now studying in the United States of America for the priesthood.

South America

The gravest difficulties raised in the whole American continent are those of the missions of South America. The primary question is: Why are there still districts in South America dependent on Propaganda? The continent is strongly Catholic, and has been for a long time. Indeed, out of a population of 175 million, 153 million are officially Catholic. But closer inspection shows that in many areas baptism is the only sacrament received by the majority of the people throughout their whole lives as Christians. The fact is that Latin America is terribly short of priests: they number only 34,000—a priest for every 4,500 Christians. There are very few native priests: what has been attempted among the Indians so far has given very poor results. Moreover, the peoples of this region are threatened by great dangers, above all the materialism sown among them by numerous anti-Catholics in the nineteenth century; then Marxism, the heir of materialism, seemingly strongly entrenched in the universities, where it wins over many young intellectuals (according to Mgr Suenens, 750 young people from South America are now undergoing indoctrination courses at Prague); and finally, numerous Protestant sects—chiefly Pentecostals—are very active, thanks to large resources from the United States of America. Noteworthy in this respect is Bolivia, where there are more than 650 such missions; in one area, where there are twenty-three Catholic missions, there are 106 Protestant missions. They do a great deal of educational work, and have established a classical and commercial college, a school of agriculture, a theological seminary, a Bible college, eighty primary schools and many radio programmes. Added to this is laxity of life (in 1935 more than 60 per cent of births in Bolivia were illegitimate, and more than 30 per cent in Colombia and Argentina) and altogether widespread superstition, often tainted with a strong remnant of paganism, in particular, spiritism. If they are to be restored to life, the Churches of South America must have priests. Any coming from Europe have to adapt themselves, for South American missions are not like other missions: the question in South America is not one of preaching the Gospel, but of causing it to be rediscovered. Above all, these Churches need the help of lay apostles, especially in the huge parishes often to be found, with fifty or a hundred thousand parishioners. They are needed to work as teachers, instructors and guides in every field, economic, social and political; they are needed to interpret and spread the Church's social teaching.

Not all the missions found in the countries of Latin America are subject to Propaganda—remember, these are lands where Catholicism has long been practised. Some missions are attached to residential dioceses. Vicariates and prefectures apostolic have been established in districts far from the great centres, or where communications are difficult —in districts peopled mainly by Indians, and men of mixed race. In all these districts a single priest is in charge of 4,500 to 6,000 souls; in Bolivia, in the Chaco missions, some of whose Indians are semi-nomads, there is to be found the frightening total of one priest for 17,000 souls. Many of these districts have been created recently:[2] fifteen out of nineteen (eleven vicariates and eight prefectures) in Colombia; two (new prefectures) out of five (the three older districts are vicariates) in Ecuador; four out of six (five vicariates and one prefecture) in Peru; one vicariate out of two in Chile; two vicariates out of five in Bolivia; and the two vicariates

[2] That is, since 1945.

in Paraguay. These forty-two districts are entrusted to nineteen different institutes: the Capuchins have seven (five of them in Colombia); the Franciscans nine (four of them in Bolivia); and the local Congregation of Foreign Missions of Yarumal, four in Colombia; the Discalced Carmelites, three; and the Jesuits, Vincentians, Salesians and Dominicans, two each. In 1952, two Dominican priests of the mission of Puerto Maldonado (Peru) succeeded in making contact with the Amarakairi tribe: previously, no one had succeeded in meeting them and remaining alive. Here are two of that kind of missionary-explorer that is so much of an anachronism in most missions today. At Nuflo de Chavez in Bolivia good results have been obtained by a "reduction" in the old style, with the foundation of a colony where several hundred natives work for the mission station, which feeds them, gives them academic and religious instruction and teaches them to till the fields. Very interesting results have been obtained from another experiment: in Colombia, in districts where at least 70 per cent are illiterate, Mgr Salcedo has been giving courses by radio, with lessons in reading and agricultural and practical subjects, as well as religion. UNESCO has been very greatly interested in the results obtained, and proposes to use the method on a large scale in all countries where illiteracy is an important problem.

OCEANIA

Australia and New Zealand must be considered separately from the rest of the area: the hierarchy has been established there for many years and they are linked with Propaganda only by a legal fiction. The two countries are divided into thirty-two districts: eight archdioceses, twenty-one dioceses, one abbey *nullius*, one vicariate apostolic and one mission *sui juris*. The remainder of Oceania (the Islands) was, in 1959, divided into twenty vicariates and a prefecture. During the year 1959 three new vicariates were brought into being in New Guinea and one in the Solomon Islands, so that the archipelago now has three instead of two, and New Guinea eight instead of five.

New Caledonia

The first attempts to evangelize New Caledonia date from 1843, under the direction of Mgr Douarre. After two setbacks, missionaries finally succeeded in establishing themselves in 1852. In 1874, after twenty years of missionary endeavour, they had succeeded in establishing a native community of 9,000 baptized Catholics and 3,000 catechumens, and there were thirty-four missionaries at work at twenty-two stations. In 1953, a hundred years after the island became French, there were 16,000 Catholics (and a further 20,000 of European origin). The island is a vicariate with forty-six priests (forty-four European Marists, and two native secular priests ordained in 1946); they are assisted by sixty-nine brothers, seventeen of them natives, and three hundred sisters, of whom eighty-nine are natives. Eight of the thirty-three mission stations on the island are without a resident priest. There are 134 churches and chapels and 198 catechists. The sixty-two schools are attended by 1,653 European pupils and 3,441 native children.

New Guinea

Once a German and Dutch colony, New Guinea is now politically divided into three regions: the west, still Dutch despite Indonesian claims, the south-east, an Australian possession, and the north-east, an Australian mandated territory. From the religious point of view, distinction must be made between coastal missions entrusted to priests of the Society of the Divine Word, and missions in the interior, entrusted to the Missionaries of the Sacred Heart of Issoudun: these latter are the missions to the Papuans. The country is very difficult, and has not yet all been explored; the natives of the interior have not advanced beyond the Stone Age and some tribes still practise cannibalism. Evangelization is difficult because the commandments are radically opposed to local customs and morals. Even after conversion the Papuan keeps his ancient stock of superstition and finds it difficult to bend to the demands of the Christian religion for daily prayer and attendance at Sunday Mass. The Papuan mission of the Fathers of the Sacred Heart is divided into twelve districts, one for each of the chief languages—there are more than two hundred languages in New Guinea altogether; each district has three priests and a school under the direction of sisters. Help from a catechist is an absolute necessity if one is to be successful in any way whatsoever. After sixty-seven years of endeavour, there are 25,000 baptized Christians out of a total population of 55,000 souls. Their faith is rather superficial, but a minority of them seem to be on the right path for the first native priest was ordained in 1953.

On the coast, too, the missions have experienced difficulties. Two missionaries were murdered in the early days of the mission. Difficulties of communications are not the least of the obstacles to be overcome and nowadays an aeroplane is the indispensable property of each mission station. Several air accidents, and the effects of war, decimated the missions. The vicar apostolic, Mgr Lorks, was executed by the Japanese, and on February 6th, 1944, Wewak was machine-gunned, taking the lives of fifty-four missionaries and nuns, including Mgr Wolf, the vicar apostolic. After the war a new start had to be made from nothing. The presence of American priests benefited the mission: the Allies left behind important material, so making possible the reconstruction of mission stations. In 1953, in all the coastal missions together, there were 70,000 Catholics in a population of more than 500,000 souls. A hundred priests spend themselves without counting the cost in a harsh apostolate and an

enervating climate; in many places mountains are still un-
explored; means of transport are costly and dangerous. The
Fathers of the Society of the Divine Word have published a
collection of hymns to native tunes: a concrete example of
what was asked for in Pius XII's Instructions on native
religious music.

Other missions in Oceania

Although less spectacular, the other missions to Oceania
offer just as many difficulties and demand no less effort. The
climate, with its tornadoes and typhoons, is sometimes a for-
midable adversary: in 1952, one of them, ravaging the Fiji
and Solomon Islands, totally destroyed two mission stations
on the island of Guadalcanal, causing as much havoc as
hostilities throughout the war. Nevertheless, there is good
cause for satisfaction in this part of Oceania: two Solomon
Islanders and four Melanesians received ordination to the
priesthood in 1953. On the other hand, vocations seem slow
in appearing in the Gilbert Islands: although the natives are
a racially superior type to the Papuans, they are too fond of
an easy life. However, a congregation of native nuns was
begun in 1952 and, in the same year, there were three minor
seminarians from the Gilbert Islands in the Fiji Islands—the
encouraging first-fruits of a Christian maturity a little slow
in appearing.

In the field of social work, we should notice the interesting
experiment of a school for housewife-catechists opened in
the Gilbert Islands. But it is principally in the sphere of
public health work that missionaries—and especially nuns—
test their devotion. Oceania is one of the regions of the world
most heavily infected with leprosy. It was in this area, at
the leper colony of Molokai in the Hawaiian Islands (a place
beyond the scope of this book, as it is not subject to Propaganda), that Fr Damien gave himself to the unhappy people
infected by this disease, finally making the supreme sacrifice

for them. Here, too, the results obtained by the use of modern therapeutics made it possible to close the leper colony on Wallace Island in 1957.

Indonesia

Catholicism has long been known here: St Francis Xavier came sowing the seed of the Word at Amboina, Ternate and in the Morean Islands. But Moslems and Dutch Calvinists wiped out the strong Christian communities of some hundred thousand souls here at the end of the sixteenth century. It was only in the middle years of the nineteenth century that the Dutch government permitted the free practice of Catholic worship in the Sunda Islands. The first attempts to preach the Gospel to the natives were made in the last years of that century. The work of the teaching and nursing orders has achieved excellent results: today there are 1,337 primary schools with 228,000 pupils; 164 secondary schools with 23,500 pupils; 37 teaching training colleges with 2,640 students; 81 vocational schools with 5,700 pupils; 52 hospitals employing 1,468 people and 103 general clinics, apart from schools of nursing and midwifery.

In forty years of missionary work there has been built up a Catholic community a million strong (a number equal to that of Protestants, whose missions have long benefited from Dutch governmental support and subsidies). Of the twenty-one vicariates (and six prefectures) three have been given to natives, the first of whom Mgr Soegijapranata, vicar apostolic of Samarang, and a member of the Society of Jesus, was nominated in 1940. The majority of the Catholics are to be found on the smaller islands; only 300,000 of them live on Java and Sumatra, the two most important islands. Although the Catholic religion now enjoys complete freedom, there are still a number of difficulties—in the first place, the entry of foreign missionaries has been almost stopped, though a tiny number of visas has been granted in the last few years.

To be able to devote themselves to the training of a stable native clergy, twelve Dutch vicars apostolic have taken Indonesian nationality and so have succeeded in staying. The increase in population is making itself felt just as much in the rural areas as in the towns, which are growing at a phenomenal rate. As the standard of living is fairly low, the whole of this mass of people is a tempting prey for Communism working through the two and a half million Chinese who have 20 per cent of the nation's income at their command. Then, too, a diehard Moslem movement tried to restrict Catholic religious activity in the first days of independence: it is now politically isolated and is almost incapable of further activity. In the sphere of social work, the Indonesian Church is actively engaged in spreading the Church's teaching. It has seen many signs of sympathy with its work, and several times has benefited from the presence of prominent Catholics in the various governments. A large part of the Catholic community is made up of the political and intellectual leaders of this young nation, a fact auguring well for the future.[3]

AFRICA

Undoubtedly to the historian of the future the year 1960 will be "the year of Africa", for during that year, reaching its majority after a rapid evolution spread over only a few decades, the black continent saw the birth of a group of new nations which, once the critical stage in their growth is passed, will be able to play a determining rôle in the world's future. Journalists have spoken of Africa as a "witches' cauldron", and it is true that forces of evil hitherto safely kept in check might now escape in free Africa. By their position and unity African Catholics alone can prevent the

[3] Propaganda puts Indonesia among the countries of South-east Asia, so that the figures compiled by Propaganda for this area include the data for Indonesia.

breaking of a storm disastrous for the whole world. The importance of the African problem did not escape Pius XII: he devoted to black Africa one of his Encyclicals, *Fidei donum* (April 21st, 1957)—an Encyclical which has become one of his most famous both because of the importance of the problems with which it is concerned and because of its loftiness of teaching.

At the beginning of 1959 there were in Africa, in the territories subject to Propaganda, twenty-eight archdioceses, ninety-eight dioceses, three abbeys *nullius*, fifty-eight vicariates and forty prefectures. But since that time far-reaching changes have been made, chiefly by the establishment of the hierarchy in the Congo and Ruanda Urundi, Northern Rhodesia and Nyasaland, and in the creation of new dioceses and prefectures. At present, if our figures are correct, there are thirty-nine archdioceses, 137 dioceses, ten vicariates and forty-one prefectures.

At the end of 1957, there were a total of 17,700,000 African Catholics, and more than 3,000,000 catechumens in a population of 168 million. (These figures do not include totals for territories not dependent on Propaganda, where there are 3,500,000 Catholics in a population of 60 million). Progress since 1920 has been remarkable. At that time in the whole of Africa there w.re 1,930,000 Catholics out of a total population of 140 million. In 1940, there were 7,115,000 Catholics in a population of 172 million; in 1955, 17,740,000 Catholics in a population of 223 million; nad in 1959, 23,200,000 in a population of 228 million. Between 1920 and 1957, the proportion increased from 1·4 per cent to 10·2 per cent. (In the areas under Propaganda alone the proportion reaches as high as 12·4 per cent.) Since 1954, three-quarters of all adult baptisms have been administered in Africa. In the attainment of these wonderful results the influence of Catholic schools has certainly not been negligible, and the efforts made by missions in the scholastic field have been enormous.

Christian development has not gone on at the same pace in every part of Africa, for the great obstacle to its progress is Islam. When an African community begins to call itself Moslem, it shuts itself off from Christian influence altogether, however recent its conversion and however rudimentary its faith. There is, then, a very good reason for the fact that in the traditionally Moslem countries of the north—Egypt and Morocco—the presence of Christianity has only prestige value: almost the only Catholics in these countries are Europeans; converted natives are very rare. This disparity between the north and other regions is clearly shown when we relate the number of Catholics to the total population district by district.

North-west Africa

In the statistics published by Propaganda this region is taken to include the following countries: Libya, Morocco and the Sahara.

In Libya there are three vicariates (Tripoli, Benghazi and Derna) and a prefecture (Misurata). All these districts except the vicariate of Tripoli (which dates back to 1643, the time of the Barbary States) were created in 1939, the time of the Italian attempt at intensive colonization. Since 1949 the number of Catholics has fallen from 53,700 to 41,300.

In Morocco there are two archdioceses (those of Tangier and Rabat, both former vicariates, created in 1650 and 1923 respectively). Since independence, proselytizing has stopped and the number of Catholics decreased, owing to the exodus of Europeans. In 1949 there were 420,800, as against 499,200 in 1953.

The Sahara comprises a diocese (Laghouat, replacing the old vicariate of Gardia dating back as a mission *sui juris* to 1901) and a prefecture (Ifni) in the Spanish Sahara. In these two districts there are 74,000 Catholics.

North-east Africa

This territory comprises Somaliland, southern Ethiopia (northern Ethiopia and Eritrea are subject to the Congregation for the Eastern Church) and the Sudan (formerly Anglo-Egyptian Sudan).

Ethiopia as defined above comprises two vicariates (Gimma and Harar) and two prefectures (Hosanna and Negelli) all entrusted to one apostolic administrator, a Capuchin. Out of a population of more than seven million, about 27,000 are Catholics (an increase of about 10 per cent in ten years); on June 30th, 1959, there were in addition 3,150 catechumens. The mission has fifty-three priests, eleven brothers, seventy-one sisters and forty-five catechists.

In Somaliland there are about 8,000 Catholics, almost all Europeans: Islam is very strongly rooted here, and has close links with nearby Arabia. However, at the end of June 1959 there were 158 catechumens. Djibouti has been a diocese since 1955, and comes under the apostolic delegation at Dakar. Mogadishu is a vicariate.

In 1949 there were in the Sudan 78,000 Catholics; today there are almost 250,000 and more than 19,000 catechumens, distributed through four vicariates (Bahr-el-Gebel; Bahr-el-Gazal; Khartoum and Rumbek), and two prefectures (Malakal and Mopoi). The vicariate of Rumbek, created in 1955, has been entrusted to a native prelate. There are 202 priests; and on June 30th, 1959, there were forty-five major seminarians, 114 brothers, 297 nuns and 1,046 catechists. All the glory for these remarkable figures must be given to the priests of the African Missions of Verona, who are in charge of almost the whole country, save for the vicariate of Khartoum, entrusted to the Society for Foreign Missions of Mill Hill.

West Africa

West Africa is certainly one of the finest jewels in the crown of the Catholic missions. Since the beginning of this century the number of Catholics has increased fortyfold. The region includes the States of what were formerly French West Africa, Togoland, Guinea, Liberia, Gambia, Sierra Leone, Ghana and Nigeria. It was with this region that the Encyclical *Fidei donum* (April 21st, 1957) was concerned.

In 1900 there were in former French West Africa 21,680 Catholics, with 130 priests, seven of them natives. In 1937, there were 121,394 Catholics (7,914 of them Europeans), with 191 priests, of whom only three were natives. In 1954, the number of Catholics had increased to 732,119 (of whom 77,304 were Europeans) with 815 priests, of whom ninety-two were natives. In 1959, there were 1,010,946 baptized Catholics and 198,616 catechumens, 1,072 priests (of whom 163 were natives) and 4,294 catechists. Of the seven archdioceses, three were entrusted to African prelates (those of Cotonu, Abijan and Uagadugu) as also were two dioceses (Ziguinchor in Senegal and Kupela in Volta) out of thirteen. Nine prefectures completes the list of districts to date. The activity in some areas is remarkable: with 131,000 baptized Catholics, the Volta Republic has more than 50,000 catechumens. In the diocese of 'N'Zerekore (in Guinea) there are 4,073 catechumens and only 3,767 baptized Catholics; in that of Nuna, there are 15,234 catechumens to 26,375 baptized Catholics; in this single diocese there are 30 per cent of Volta's catechumens and—the one fact explains the other—an equally remarkable number of catechists (382 to forty-four priests, a ratio of nine to one). It is therefore not surprising that the number of Catholics in the country has tripled in ten years. In 1949 there were sixteen Volta-born priests; by 1949, the number had increased to forty-five. Equally flattering results are to be credited to the Dahomey mission where the number of Catholics increased from 112,000 in 1949 to 238,000 in 1959—166,000 in the single archdiocese of Cotonu alone, where there are also 22,000 of the 36,000 catechumens. In the prefecture of Paraku, although there are only 10,430 baptized Catholics, there are 7,348 catechumens: its twenty-seven priests are assisted by 137 catechists (a ratio of five to one). In the diocese of Porto Novo, the proportion is even greater: there are 160 catechists to twenty priests. On the Ivory Coast, too, the number of Catholics has practically doubled in the last ten years, rising from 124,000 to 236,000; in three dioceses (Daloa, Buake and Katiola) out of five, there are more than half as many catechumens as there are baptized Catholics. At Buaka, there are 190 catechists for thirty-one priests. Sixty per cent of all the Catholics in the country live in the archdiocese of Abijan. Notice too the remarkable work of the twenty White Fathers and twenty-five catechists in the prefecture of Gao (Sudan) where there is an estimated number of 1,313 baptized Catholics and 5,256 catechumens in one of the areas of the old French African Empire most strongly influenced by Islam. We might go on to quote numerous similar cases. We have already referred to the uneven distribution of Catholics in the various districts of Togoland: in the archdiocese of Lome there are 181,000 baptized Catholics and 14,000 catechumens in a population of 515,000 (i.e. 38 per cent); in the diocese of Sokode there are only 18,000 Catholics and 14,000 catechumens among the 592,000 inhabitants (5·7 per cent). Here too the labourers are far too few: although there are sixty-four priests and 344 catechists in Lome, there are only thirty-two priests and ninety-four catechists in Sokode.

There is, however, one great cause for hope: the remarkable increase in the total of native clergy (163 priests as against fifty-one ten years ago, and five bishops and archbishops) seems likely to continue for in 1959 there were 106 students at major seminaries. Nevertheless, this number is still too few and much remains to be done.

Guinea, however, casts a shadow over the scene. The Marxist influence was very strong when this State was born. President Sekou Touré began his political training under the

General Confederation of Labour and finished it behind the
Iron Curtain. These are facts which make the future look
disquieting. The government of Guinea has already made two
attempts to nationalize the mission schools; in the face of the
opposition they aroused, it did not persist in them, but is
now trying to gain its ends through a system of subsidies
making it possible for it to intervene by gradually forcing its
own teachers on schools, so stifling them. It hopes to have
liquidated them within three years. A redoubling of effort
will be necessary—especially in the social field—if the spread
of the Marxist infection is to be prevented: this involves an
increase in the number of schools of all grades, the firm
implantation of the various branches of Catholic Action, the
youth movements and the Legion of Mary, the giving of
support to help the spread of active Christian trade unionism,
the expansion of the Catholic Press and, in the sphere of the
propagation of the faith, continual advance, always bearing
in mind that Islam is advancing three times as fast as Catholicism in the areas still to be won.

Among the other countries of West Africa as defined by
Propaganda undoubtedly the most important are Nigeria and
Ghana. Nigeria has 1,676,400 Catholics in the population of
33,000,000: in 1949 there were no more than 656,000 Catholics. The increase has been remarkable—in the region of
10 per cent a year. The country is divided into four archdioceses, nine dioceses and five prefectures. Two dioceses
(Lagos and Onicha) and two dioceses (Omuahia and Calabar)
have been entrusted to Nigerian prelates. In 1959 a census
showed 556,000 catechumens, 776 priests, 133 major seminarians, 117 brothers, 452 nuns and 11,432 catechists (6,152
of them in the archdiocese of Onicha and 2,542 in the diocese
of Ogoja).

In Ghana there are 563,000 Catholics and more than
94,000 catechumens in a population of 4,800,000 people.
There are 281 priests, forty-nine of them natives. The country

is divided into six ecclesiastical districts: one archdiocese (Cape Coast) entrusted to the local clergy, and five dioceses, one of them, Accra, with a Ghanaian bishop. Ten years ago Catholics numbered 293,000, and native priests, nineteen. There are great hopes for this country; but there is one weak spot: there are still not enough catechists, for there are only 970 of them, only four to each priest, whilst in Nigeria there are fifteen to each priest.

Undoubtedly the poorest results have come from work in Gambia and Sierra Leone, although it is true that Islam is strong in both countries (275,000 of the 285,000 inhabitants of Gambia are Moslems, and 1,750,000 of the 2,080,000 inhabitants of Sierra Leone). In 1959 there were in Gambia 4,721 baptized Catholics and 625 catechumens; together they formed a diocese with thirteen priests: none of these was a native, neither were there any major seminarians. There were only thirty-three catechists. (In 1949 Catholics numbered 2,600: an increase of only 5 per cent a year). In Sierra Leone Catholics numbered 18,545 in 1959, as against 9,600 ten years earlier. The single diocese of Freetown contains 16,000 of the baptized Catholics, 17,300 of the 20,000 catechumens, forty-seven of the sixty-one priests and sixty of the seventy catechists. Hope is greater in this country than in Gambia, for there is already one native priest, and a major seminarian. The prefecture of Makene, created in 1952 and entrusted to the Society of St Francis Xavier of Parma, already has a strength of 4,000 Catholics (as against 600 at the beginning of 1955) and 2,700 catechumens: fourteen priests and ten catechists are doing some notable work there.

Liberia, an independent state founded in 1843 by an American Anti-Slavery Society, in the beginning had 40,000 Protestants. Islam, however, has not yet penetrated into the country, and 96 per cent of the population are still to be won. There is a wonderful field for Catholic missionary endeavour here, but progress has been slow: there are now

12,800 baptized Catholics as against 4,800 ten years ago, and there are still 1,200,000 souls to be won. There is a vicariate, and a prefecture, with thirty-nine priests (one a native) and six major seminarians, ninety-five catechists, and only a thousand catechumens. Here, too, the shortage of priests is painfully obvious.

Central Africa

According to Propaganda, Central Africa comprises the countries of what was once French Equatorial Africa, together with the Cameroons, Spanish Guinea, Fernando Po, the Congo, Ruanda and Urundi. This is a region where the faith seems to have taken firm root in many places: more than 20 per cent of the population of the Cameroons is Catholic and 34 per cent of that of the Congo, Ruanda and Urundi taken together, and 55½ per cent of that of Gabon. The faith is very much alive (more than 50 per cent of Catholics in the Cameroons made their Easter duties and progress is continuing: in Ruanda, a brake has had to be put on baptisms, because there are not enough priests to permit the founding of new parishes). Here, too, as in West Africa, there is a general shortage of pastors.

The Cameroons' first missionaries arrived during the German occupation; but with the events of 1914–18 the rate of evangelization seemed to slow. It picked up again with the French mandate and has progressed remarkably well: in 1949 there were already close on 480,000 baptized Catholics; ten years later a count showed 702,820 Catholics and 93,172 catechumens in a total population of 3,200,000. The country is divided into one archdiocese (Yaunde) and four dioceses (Duala, 'N'Kongsamba, Dume and Garua) and has only 453 priests, 120 of them natives. The archdiocese of Yaunde has a Cameronian auxiliary bishop and the diocese of Duala has been entrusted to a native bishop. There are also forty-nine students at major seminaries, 170 religious who are not priests, 473 sisters and 5,414 catechists.

The countries formerly comprising French Equatorial Africa show very diverse characteristics as far as evangelization is concerned. Gaboon can be proud of itself: in 1959 there were 185,000 baptized Catholics and 31,500 catechumens in a population of 400,000; by way of contrast, in Chad, there were only 54,000 baptized Catholics (and, it is true, 50,000 catechumens) in a population of 2,573,000 souls. The Congolese Republic had a population of 766,000 inhabitants with 258,000 Catholics and 24,000 catechumens. The Central African Republic (formerly Ubangi-Shari) had only 126,000 Catholics and 44,000 catechumens in a population of 1,135,000. These territories are together divided into three archdioceses (Libreville, Brazzaville and Bangui), six dioceses and three prefectures. Seven districts are entrusted to the Holy Ghost Fathers, three to the Capuchins, one to the Jesuits and one to the Oblates of Mary Immaculate. There are forty-four native priests ready to relieve them (an increase of seventeen in ten years) and thirty-one major seminarians. 144 brothers and 457 nuns assist them ably, together with 4,551 catechists. The increase in the number of those baptized is steady: 20,000 a year between 1949 and 1955 and 35,000 a year since that date.

On reaching the Congo (formerly the Belgian Congo) we enter one of those countries that has recently reached its religious majority. Together with Ruanda and Urundi, the hierarchy was set up here on November 10th, 1959. At that time there was a force of 4,865,800 baptized Catholics and 604,000 catechumens. This proportion of one Catholic in eight inhabitants, however, shows considerable variation from one district to another. In ten years the number of Catholics has practically doubled, as it has throughout black Africa: indeed, the census in 1949 gave a figure of 2,550,000 Catholics. The number of priests at work in 1959 was 2,776 of whom 389 were Congolese (as against 154 in 1949); 342 students at major seminaries were preparing to go to the help of a missionary force that is always too small (there is one priest for every 1,850 Catholics, the average figure throughout black Africa). Auxiliary forces include 1,212 brothers, 3,747 sisters and 31,443 catechists (an average of eight to each priest). Average figures should not, however, be allowed to mislead us: there are considerable variations from diocese to diocese. The new ecclesiastical division of the country comprises six archdioceses, twenty-six dioceses and seven prefectures. Two new archdioceses and three new dioceses have been created since the end of 1959, bringing the total number of ecclesiastical districts up to forty-four. Several contemplative orders have established foundations in the Congo, and are enjoying a remarkable measure of success among the natives.

Ruanda and Urundi, former German colonies now administered by Belgium under a mandate, are probably the two countries where endeavours in recent years to spread the faith have enjoyed the most extraordinary success. At the beginning of the century there was not a single Catholic in either country; in 1920 there were still only 35,000; today there are about two million in a population of four million (the actual figures are 1,956,000 Catholics and 460,000 catechumens). There are 525 priests, 169 of them native, and two native bishops. The hierarchy—established on November 10th, 1959—has divided the two countries into two archdioceses and three dioceses. There are now 239 major seminarians, 691 sisters and 4,671 catechists. The instruction of catechumens is very thorough, lasting at least four years, with a probationary period of one to two years. It is thought that within a year or two, 60 per cent of the population will have been baptized. The Christian zeal of this people is wonderful, with an average of twenty Communions for every adult every year. These results were made possible by the moral purity of the pagans and their belief in the existence of a supreme God, without either fetishism or idolatry, although they have a great number of superstitions. Almost all the regional chiefs have been baptized. This is another area of huge parishes—up to three hundred square miles—with 30,000 to 50,000 parishioners and needing division into five or six sub-districts with chapels and thirty or forty chapel-schools entrusted to the keeping of catechists. There are both Protestant and Moslem missions, the Moslems being Ismailis from Zanzibar and Tanganyika. At the present time, 70,000 pupils are attending mission schools.

South Africa

South Africa, according to the system of geography adopted by Propaganda, comprises the Union of South Africa properly so called, South-west Africa (once a German colony) and the British Protectorates of Basutoland, Bechuanaland and Swaziland. In all these countries together there are 1,206,500 Catholics in a total population of a little over fifteen million, about half of whom are Protestants. The 61,000 catechumens represent a proportion of only 5 per cent of the number of baptized Catholics—a very low figure for Africa. The lowest percentage occurs in Natal, with only 8,650 catechumens and 322,650 baptized Catholics; the highest is to be found in what was formerly the Orange Free State (9,816 to 78,580). In the last ten years progress has been slower in this area than in the rest of Black Africa.

Together all these countries form four archdioceses (all in the Union of South Africa), seventeen dioceses, two vicariates, and four prefectures, together with one abbey *nullius* (a Benedictine foundation at Pietersburg). The four archbishops and two of the bishops of the Union of South Africa are whites born in South Africa—a fact making even more precious their courageous protests against the policy of racial segregation pursued by the South African government. One of the sees in the province of Natal, and another in Basutoland are entrusted to Negro bishops. The number of major seminarians is not much above a hundred (108 to be precise). There are also about 700 brothers and 5,500 nuns; catechists number 3,100, of whom 1,230 live in Basutoland and 1,700 in the four provinces of the Union of South Africa.

East Africa

Included in this sub-division are the Rhodesian Federation and Nyasaland, Kenya, Tanganyika and Uganda. The total population of these countries is about twenty-eight million. Catholics number a little more than five million, and the rate of increase is remarkable, being in some districts comparable to that in Ruanda and Urundi: in ten years Southern Rhodesia has seen the number of its baptized Catholics increase from 80,000 to 224,000; in the same period the number in Kenya increased from 325,000 to 764,000. In Uganda where, eighty years ago, the first converts were burned, there are now more than 1,700,000 Catholics (and more than 72,000 catechumens) in a total population of 5,680,000 souls. Altogether there are a little over 600,000 catechumens in all these lands together (or about 12 per cent of the population—still a modest figure compared with some parts of Central and West Africa).

2,840 priests devote themselves to the Catholics of these areas and to the souls still to be saved there; 564 of their number are native priests—a noteworthy proportion. In ten years their number has doubled. There are more than 400 major seminarians. There are grounds for great hopes in Tanganyika and Uganda. Seven districts have been entrusted to bishops native to the country: in Kenya, the diocese of Kisii, created on May 21st, 1960, with 100,000 Catholics in a population of 720,000, has been given to Mgr Otunga who, at the age of thirty-seven, is one of the youngest bishops in the world.

The Islands

This division includes in the Indian Ocean, Madagascar and its dependencies, Réunion, Mauritius and the Seychelles, and in the Gulf of Guinea the Spanish possessions together forming the diocese of Fernando Po (the islands of Annobon, Corisco, Elobey and Fernando Po, together with the Rio Muni territory on the mainland). This last see has 192,800 Catholics and 14,000 catechumens in a population of about 400,000: there are fifty-five priests, fourteen of them native (in 1949 there were four). They are helped by 353 catechists, twenty-nine religious and 159 sisters. There are also ten students in major seminaries.

In the Seychelles there is only one native priest, although virtually the whole of the population of the archipelago is Catholic (approximately 38,000 out of 40,000) and although the capital, Port Victoria, was made a diocese in 1892.

Although it is a department of France, Reunion, like the French West Indies, is subject to Propaganda. Made a see in 1850 and entrusted to the Holy Ghost Fathers, the island has 300,000 Catholics in a population of 310,000, ninety-one priests (thirty-seven of them native), seven major seminarians and 868 catechists. The difficulties arising here are almost the same as those in the West Indies: the existence of very rigid divisions made according to differences of colour, low moral standard among the common people, intermittent unemployment (there is a one-crop economy, based on sugar cane), malnutrition, alcoholism: in short a vast field for social work.

Mauritius, a British possession, where French is the common language, is also an old see, having been founded in 1847. Catholics number 200,000 in a population of 580,000 (it has grown 30 per cent in the last ten years). The bishop is assisted by seventy-eight priests (thirty-six of them native), twenty-two brothers, 295 sisters and 249 catechists; fourteen major seminarians are at present preparing to reinforce the ranks of the missionaries.

Madagascar, "the Large Island", dominates the whole of this region with its 1,091,244 Catholics in a population of 5,100,000. Progress in the last ten years has been excellent —in 1949 a census showed only 700,000 Catholics, and one in 1954 only 900,000. The island is divided into three archdioceses and twelve dioceses (the most recent of them— Morombe—having been made in May 1960 by cutting off part of the diocese of Morondava). One archdiocese (Tananarive) and a diocese (Miarinarivo) are entrusted to native prelates. 603 priests (146 of them Madagascans) devote themselves to the service of this fine community. They are helped by 5,800 catechists, 451 brothers and 934 sisters. There is a firm and already old tradition behind the Madagascan native clergy: the first native was ordained in 1911, fifty years ago. It will be recalled that the first native bishop was consecrated in 1939 by Pius XII himself: he was Mgr Ramarosandratana and was given the vicariate of Miarinarivo. In some parts of the island (especially in the archdiocese of Diego Suarez) there are serious obstacles in the way of missionary work. They have two main causes: the wide dispersal of the population and difficulty of communications on the one hand, and Communist propaganda on the other. Nonetheless, throughout the island Catholic social action is progressing, whether in the form of Catholic Action, or that of Christian trade unions. The success of youth movements is very encouraging.

ASIA

Catholics in the vast continent of Asia may seem lost in the midst of Buddhist, Hindu and Moslem populations. Indeed, there are scarcely more than thirteen millions of them (of whom five millions are living under Communist rule of the most rigid kind, and together constitute the Silent Church, of which we shall speak later), in a population of 1,300 millions. They stand face to face with 300 million Buddhists,

400 million Chinese Confucians, 300 million Hindus and 250 million Moslems. It is quite impossible to penetrate into the Communist countries and Afghanistan; the Himalayan states are hardly open. Huge problems of every kind have been raised by the scale of the exodus of those from China and North Vietnam who have succeeded in escaping from the "Red Paradise". There is a native clergy, and everywhere it is of high quality, but everywhere its numbers are too few to take on all the necessary tasks. The bishops of the Far East, meeting in conference in December 1958, based great hopes on success achieved in social work and on the lay apostolate.

West Asia—together with the Indian dioceses of the Syrian Rite—is subject to the Sacred Congregation for the Eastern Church: the rest of Asia is divided by Propaganda into three main areas: Southern Asia, South-east Asia and Eastern Asia.

Southern Asia

This area is made up of India, Pakistan, Ceylon, the Maldive Archipelago and the Himalayan states of Bhutan and Nepal. At the end of 1955 there were in the area 5,250,000 Catholics, in a total population of 500 million. A census in 1920 showed 2,350,000 in a population of 326 million, and one in 1940, 3,590,000 in 410 million. The increase in the number of Catholics of the Latin Rite has been quite remarkable in the last fifteen years. Their spiritual lives are guided by 4,900 priests (an increase of more than 10 per cent in four years), 3,182 of them Asiatics and 1,720 foreigners (348 Italians, 257 French, 253 Belgians, etc.). To these totals must be added those for the Christians of the Eastern Rite (Syro-Malabars and Syro-Malankars) in India, of whom there are one million, and the 400,000 Goan Catholics, subject to the Patriarchate of Lisbon and to the Consistory.

The creation of the Moslem State of Pakistan led to fears that there would be set up there a theocratic régime, where the Catholic religion would be banned, and missionaries not allowed to enter. Fortunately nothing of the sort has occurred. It is a strange land with no natural frontier and two capitals—Karachi and Dacca—as far apart as Madrid and Warsaw. Despite the mischief made by a small faction of fanatics, the Catholic Church has become remarkably stronger here after twelve years of endeavour: there are now more than 300,000 Catholics in this country of 78 million people, most of them in the lower classes, although there has also appeared a superior class of officials, who may later be a great help. The liberal outlook of the party in power has made possible the growth of Christian schools: the only condition is that they must accept all children, including young Moslems. An obligation to teach the Koran exists only on paper. Social work is developing on a vast scale: the country has been endowed with five ultra-modern Christian hospitals and 365 schools attended by more than 50,000 pupils, as well as seven university colleges. Political changes might imperil the toleration the Church now enjoys: it is therefore important that she should send down deep roots, and the training of a native clergy is a necessity. The first native priest was ordained in 1956. He was a native of East Pakistan. Four others, natives of the Punjab, were ordained in 1960, and five more are expected to be ordained in 1961, and forty-seven in 1962. There is one archdiocese in each of the provinces (Karachi and Dacca), each with three suffragan bishops. The hierarchy was established in 1950; 335 priests work here, eighty-two Asiatics and 253 foreigners.

To some extent India is a country with an old Christian tradition, for the Church is said to have been founded here by the apostle St Thomas himself and is thus the mother Church of the Syrian rite still extant today. Catholicism was brought into the country in the fifteenth century by Portuguese colonists and advanced chiefly through the missionary work of St Francis Xavier, the second Apostle of India. Its main growth came, however, with the nineteenth-century missions, making it possible for Leo XIII to establish the hierarchy there in 1886. The one special difficulty in the way of missionary work in India is the age-old social system, the caste system, now theoretically abolished by the Constitution, but kept alive by custom. Missionaries since Fr de Nobili, S.J., at the beginning of the seventeenth century, have been seeking a solution to it. Nevertheless, although in some periods and places slowed down by the caste barriers, the advance of the Catholic religion has been quite remarkable. In 1871 there were 786,000 baptized Catholics; twenty years later, the number had increased to 1,300,000; in 1920 it was 2,400,000, and in 1957 close on 5,400,000. The rate of growth today is in the order of 3,500 a year, while India's population is growing by three million a year. The country is divided into thirteen archdioceses and forty-one dioceses; nine arch-bishops and twenty-one bishops are natives of the country and Mgr Gracias, archbishop of Bombay, was made a cardinal in January 1953. In the districts subject to Propaganda there are more than 3,500 priests, of whom about 2,000 are natives. The sixty major seminaries and religious training centres have more than 2,000 students. Geographically, however, Catholics are very unevenly distributed: figures published in 1947 show that in the northern states, occupying more than two-thirds of the land area of the Union, there are only 750,000 Catholics in a total population of 220 million; in the southern states there are 3,500,000 in a population of 140 million. At that time there was in the north one priest to 920 Catholics and 35,000 non-Catholics. In northern and Central India, the Church has come into collision with a very active Hindu revival: one party—Hindu Mahasaba—would like to set up a theocratic state in Central India, but it has received no support from Pandit Nehru's very tolerant government. On the local scale, the Church has sometimes suffered by the sharp practices of petty officials: these have, however, always been disowned by New Delhi.

Special efforts have been made to establish the religious life firmly in India. In 1950, there were more than 7,000 native sisters among the 11,000 working in the country. Fr Montchanin and Dom Lesault, O.S.B., have tried to bring into being an Indian congregation, on the pattern of that founded in China by Fr Lebbe. In 1951, a congregation of nuns was founded at Calcutta with the special object of working among the poor in the slums.

But the most important problems arising in India are social. Overpopulation has led the central government to support birth control and family limitation. The Church, however, being opposed to artificial limitation of any kind, has undertaken a campaign against the policy of birth control— a campaign which has not always been understood. But her most systematic work has been the fight against the caste system. The Indian bishop of Guntur (part of Hyderabad) has said that it will take more than a year or two to stamp it out. It has sometimes hindered the spread of Catholicism, and Catholicism has had to adjust itself to it. Upper-class Hindus have often claimed that Catholicism is a religion meant only for outcasts. Ignorance has sometimes led to their scornful opinion being shared in the West. It is true that on the Malabar Coast, where there are seven dioceses and 650,000 Catholics of the Latin Rite (as against eight dioceses and 1,800,000 Christians of the Syrian Rite), many of the Catholics belong to the poor classes, being mostly fishermen; furthermore, the majority of the people in this region have a fairly low standard of living and give a ready ear to the Marxists. Indeed, the State of Kerala, for a time the first Communist government in India, is to be found in this region: it has been claimed that Catholics here compelled people to vote Communist, but this calumny will not stand up to examination, for the first act of the Communist government was to do away with the Catholic schools; a long struggle ensued, and Catholics played a prominent part in the events leading up to the dismissal of the Communist leaders of the State by the central authorities at New Delhi. On the Coromandel Coast, the Paravers, a people dear to St Francis Xavier, through their trading activities have attained, or rather, at least some of them have attained, a comfortable standard. There are very few Christian Brahmins: they live chiefly in the province of Madura, where Fr de Nobili performed his apostolate among their seventeenth-century ancestors. There are now about three hundred of them, five of them having joined the Jesuits of Madura (for the mission has been entrusted to French Jesuits) and fourteen girls have taken the veil as nuns. In the same diocese, the Vellages— the class immediately below the Brahmins—make up about 12 per cent of the Catholic community. In the whole Tamil region there are about 110,000 of them, and from them have come more than half the 625 priests working in the eleven dioceses of the country. Untouchables are always numerous in Tamil districts, and they form a third of the population of Madura. In Telugu areas, the Reddiars—the equivalent of the Tamil Vellages—are very important: they make up almost the whole of the 45,000-strong Catholic population of the diocese of Guntur. The Gospel was preached to their forefathers by French Jesuits in the eighteenth century. Nevertheless, it is still true to say that most Catholics live in the villages, and are farmers or agricultural labourers. But there are also several tens of thousands of industrial workers who are daily subjected to intense Communist propaganda. In the big cities, such as Bombay, Madras or Calcutta, there are also many doctors and lawyers and some university professors among the faithful. Furthermore, some of the faithful have been promoted to important administrative posts: one is a collector at Trichinopoly, another a minister in the State of Madras and a third prime minster of the State of Travancore-Cochin.

The Church owes these flattering successes in large measure

to its policy in the educational field—a policy quickly taken up by the missions and all the religious Orders engaged in missionary work. The missions have devoted themselves to giving instruction of a fundamentally practical kind at the elementary stage, instruction not intended to lead the pupil automatically to entry to the secondary school. The colleges which have made Christian education famous are reserved for an upper stratum specially prepared for entry to them at "middle" schools. Two kinds of education are offered there: the first "academic" or "classical", the other, technical and semi-vocational. In 1900, Catholic education was offered in twelve university colleges, 128 high schools and 1,247 primary schools. In 1952 the figures had become forty-five colleges, 420 high schools and 4,543 primary schools, the number of pupils at colleges being 25,000 (only 20 per cent of them Catholics); at high schools, 222,000; and in the primary schools, 608,000. The four biggest of the forty-five colleges (those at Bombay, Trichinopoly, Changanachery and Madras) were under Jesuit direction. The important problem facing Catholic education is that of its relations with the government: at present, they are good—but what of the future, especially if the exclusivist Hindu Mahasaba movement succeeds in gaining power?

Another factor that has worked in favour of Catholicism is the large number and unbiased character of its social works. In the diocese of Vijayavada (in the Hyderabad area), the maternity home at Jaggayett was built in 1945 six years before the mission station; now, after less than nine years of missionary activity, the mission embraces twenty-one villages, only seven of which have their own chapels. The priest—a member of the Milan Institute for Foreign Missions—is assisted by five catechists. At the University College of Trichinopoly, volunteer students, not all of them Catholics, fill their Saturdays with health visiting in the poorest quarters, washing urchins, amusing them with team games (especially football), visiting poor families, arranging evening classes for adults and operating a system of milk distribution to undernourished children. Theirs is a wonderful example of that kind of concrete action which pours scorn on the ancient prejudices of the caste system.

Ceylon

It was the Portuguese who, in the sixteenth century, introduced the Catholic religion into Ceylon. Evangelization, stopped by the collapse of the Portuguese Empire and the Dutch occupation, was begun again in the nineteenth century. The hierarchy was established on the island in 1886—at the same time as in India—by Leo XIII. In a population of eight million, there are 800,000 Catholics, 100,000 Protestants, 500,000 Moslems, almost two million Tamil Hindus and five million Buddhists. Most of the Catholics are Tamil converts from Hinduism. The conversion rate today is very low: the increase in the number of the faithful parallels that of the population. The country comprises one archdiocese (Colombo) and six dioceses, together embracing 222 parishes. The archbishop of Colombo and three of the bishops are natives of the country, as also are more than 60 per cent of the priests, the rest being either Europeans or Asiatics (Indians or Chinese). At Colombo there is a college with about 3,000 pupils, under the direction of the Christian Brothers. The religious life has had a great success among the Singalese since Fr Joseph Vaz founded, almost clandestinely, a native congregation of Oratorians in the eighteenth century.

Catholicism encounters difficulties of two kinds, the first in the political sphere (because Communists have had places in the primarily Buddhist government since 1956); the second in the religious sphere, originating with these same Buddhists who, in the face of recent Christian successes, have become militant and aggressive, and are turning to exclusivism, hoping to proclaim Buddhism the State religion.

South-east Asia

Except for New Guinea and Indonesia—dealt with under Oceania—and the Philippines (most of which are subject to the Consistorial Congregation), this area includes most of the lands often called Buddhist, because Buddhism, the dominant religion, is the characteristic common to them all. Hence it covers Burma, Thailand (Siam), Malaya, Cambodia, Laos and Vietnam.

Buddhism is in fact the religion of 90 per cent of the population of Thailand, 83 per cent of that of Laos and of 80 per cent of that of Malaya and Cambodia. Except in Burma where, as in Ceylon, there is a revival of proselytism, Buddhism is everywhere somnolent, and is offering only light resistance to Communism.

Among Burma's population of twenty million and a half, there are 183,000 Catholics. For the last ten years, progress has been at the rate of about 5 per cent a year: in 1949 there were 131,000 baptized Catholics. More than half of those already baptized are in the archdiocese of Rangoon and the diocese of Toungoo (58,000 and 47,000 respectively), that is, in the south-eastern part of the country. The leading missionary institute is the *Missions Étrangères de Paris* (with fifty-four), heading the Milan Society for Foreign Missions (forty-seven) and the Society of St Columban (thirty-one). It should be remembered that it was missionaries who first brought a printing press to Central Burma (in 1870): it was set up in a brick building, the first ever built with this material in the district. The complexity of local tongues compelled the priests to cast special characters, formed from the Latin letters modified with accents and various additional signs. The last war led to its complete destruction and a totally new beginning had to be made.

In Thailand there is an even greater proportion of Buddhists than in Burma, and therefore Catholics are less numerous: in a population of twenty-one million, there are only 109,000 baptized Catholics and 2,500 catechumens (as against 52,500 baptized Catholics and 737 catechumens in 1953). Of the 233 priests, eighty-seven are Thai and 146 foreigners (in 1949 there were only sixty-three natives and fifty-seven foreigners). In 1949 there were only eleven major seminarians, today there are fifty-six. 447 of the 687 nuns are native to Thailand. These are very encouraging results.

Catholic schools have been gratifyingly successful, for they now teach 30,000 boys and 28,000 girls. It should be noticed that 90 per cent of their pupils are Buddhists. The teaching of Buddhism is compulsory, and more than half the teachers are laymen. It should also be noticed that the expansion of Catholicism has coincided with the influx into the country of refugees from China and North Vietnam. Nevertheless, there have been some conversions among the educated classes because the official religion is negative and tends to atheism, for the worshipper's ultimate goal is annihilation of self. The government is anti-Communist and respects Catholicism, which is arousing the interest even of orthodox Buddhist monks. Furthermore, 10,000 students (of whom only 150 are Christian) attend the five Catholic university colleges. The country now comprises five vicariates (two of which are entrusted to the local secular clergy) and one prefecture.

The other Buddhist countries offer no new special characteristics. In Malaya there are 180,000 Catholics in a population of seven million and a half. The country is divided into one archdiocese, Malacca, and two dioceses entrusted to the local clergy. In Cambodia, there are hardly 50,000 Catholics in a population of 4,900,000: the vicariate of Phnom-Penh has fifty-one priests (twenty-one Cambodians and thirty Frenchmen, all members of the *Missions Étrangères de Paris*). Laos, divided into the vicariate of Vientiane and the prefecture of Thakhek, has no more than 16,000 baptized Catholics and 2,000 catechumens in its population of a million and a half. During the war there were several cases of persecution in this country, acts either of the Japanese occupying army, or of local fanatics.

Tibet has the distinction among Buddhist countries of being the most firmly closed of them all. Between 1624 and 1745 missionaries made four attempts to penetrate into the country, but without much success. In 1845, a further attempt was made by two Vincentians, Fr Huc and Fr Gabet; they brought back almost nothing to the Christian world except a well-documented and picturesque account of their journey. The country having been finally closed to missionaries, vicariates were set up around its periphery in Chinese Turkestan (at Ta Tsien Lu) and in Sikkim. Swiss canons regular of St Maurice and of the Grand Saint-Bernard established hospices in the most frequented passes; but between 1854 and 1940, eleven missionaries paid with their lives for their attempts to enter the forbidden land. In 1949, Canon Tornay reached Lhasa. He was arrested and expelled, and was finally assassinated by his guides on his return journey. Since then, the Bamboo Curtain has fallen over the roof of the world.

Vietnam's position is a peculiar one among the countries of South-east Asia, for it was divided into North and South under the Geneva agreements of July, 1954. The northern part, abandoned to the Communists, had fifteen million inhabitants, of whom 1,100,000 were Catholics, with 1,152 priests; in the South there were then hardly 400,000 Catholics (with 704 priests) in a population of nine millions. The critical period was between 1940 and 1954 during the Japanese occupation and the war with the Communists: twenty missionaries were martyred. A special clause in the Geneva agreements allowed for unrestricted emigration of those who preferred one régime to the other. But while very few southerners went north, the following months saw the exodus of more than a million Tonkinese, half of them Catholics, to the south, despite obstacles of every kind put in their way by the Communists. Spontaneously, or on the advice of their priests, whole parishes abandoned everything—their villages, homes, fields, and even the graves of their ancestors (and it is well known how much respect men have in these lands for the tombs of their forefathers) so as to live in their faith without either fear or constraint. Even after the frontiers of Vietminh were finally closed some succeeded in escaping. It is now estimated that about 680,000 Catholics have managed to come together in the South, where they have founded 250 new villages. Other refugees have founded forty-four Buddhist villages (with about 240,000 people) and four Protestant villages (with 2,000 people). Nearly four hundred priests, with two vicars apostolic, one French coadjutor bishop and two native bishops, have stayed where they were in the North to protect what can still be saved. 617 priests and fifty monks have followed the refugees, and it proved possible to evacuate five major seminaries with 267 students, and seven minor seminaries with 85,000 pupils. At the end of 1957, the new South Vietnam had 1,100,000 Catholics, 68,000 catechumens. 1,264 priests (163 of them foreigners, 127 of them Frenchmen), 254 major seminarians, 650 brothers, 3,250 nuns and 1,672 catechists actively lending their support to missionary work. An interesting measure of success has been enjoyed by the contemplative orders: three native Cistercian monasteries have been founded: the two first, Phuocson and Chauson (founded in 1918 and 1936 respectively) are now in the Communist zone. A group of brothers (fifty of them, including the young students) succeeded at the end of 1952 in reaching the area around Saigon, from where they were able to rejoin the third house of their order, Phuocly. It should be remembered that President Ngo Dinh Diem is a Catholic and the brother of Mgr Ngo Dinh Thuc, vicar apostolic of Vinh-Long.

Eastern Asia

Twelve years ago the most flourishing Christian communities in all Asia were to be found in this region. But the

Bamboo Curtain fell in 1949, plunging 145 ecclesiastical districts into darkness and sorrow. Today there are only thirty districts (two archdioceses, ten dioceses, nine vicariates and nine prefectures). Fifteen of them are in Japan.

Japan, "God's flourishing garden" as St Francis Xavier called it, saw terrible trials between 1596, the year of the first systematic persecution, and 1865, the date of the missionaries' return. At that time there were only a few thousand Christians left around Nagasaki, among whom baptism was passed down from father to son, living without either priests or the other sacraments, but protected by a miraculous dispensation of Providence. Slowly evangelization began again: for eighty years there were never more than 120,000 baptized Catholics, 70,000 of them descendants of the Christians of Nagasaki. But it should be remembered that complete freedom to propagate the faith dates back only to 1945. Since that time the number of the faithful has rocketed: it increased from 131,000 in 1949 to 212,000 in 1955 and to 266,000 by the end of June, 1959. In ten years, it has more than doubled. The largest group—78,000—are, of course, to be found in the old diocese of Nagasaki, but in fact it is here that the least progress is being made at present: the diocese appears to have a closed mind, the "ghetto" mentality, the relic of three centuries of life in hiding.

There are now 19,700 catechumens, of whom 4,165 live in the diocese of Kyoto, where there are only 13,500 baptized Catholics. Both the archdioceses (Nagasaki and Tokyo), the nine dioceses (Fukuoka, Hiroshima, Kagoshima, Kyoto, Osaka, Sapporo, Sendai, Urawa and Yokohama) and the four prefectures (Miyazaki, Nagoya, Niigata and Shikoko) have been entrusted to Japanese prelates. The number of priests increased from 595 to 1,583 between 1949 and 1959 (these numbers include 181 and 392 Japanese respectively). In 1959 there were 237 major seminarians and 118 resident scholastics (twenty-three Jesuits, nineteen Franciscans, four-

teen Marists, twelve Conventual Franciscans, nine members
of the Society of the Holy Ghost and eight of the Society of
the Divine Word, three Redemptorists and two Carmelites).
Devoted assistance is given by 442 brothers, 4,349 sisters and
781 catechists.

What magic names there are among these Catholic
communities in Japan! Kagoshima: the first mission in the
country founded by St Francis Xavier; Nagasaki and Hiroshima, the martyred cities. What wonderful examples they
are to new converts, to those who, looking for a new ideal,
are driven inexorably towards the Catholic faith! Since the
end of the war so many of the idols of the Japan of tradi-
tionalism and fierce nationalism have fallen. MacArthur's
constitution brought about fundamental secularization of the
Japanese state: the doctrine of the semi-divine nature of the
emperor became a matter for history books and Shinto, the
official, wholly ritual, religion lost most of its worth and its
logical basis. Educated Japanese began to show a lively
interest in Christianity because of its "exotic" character: in
it they found an escape from the consequences and dis-
illusionments of the past. Protestantism, already at work
here before the war, now intensified its propaganda, profiting
from the help given it by the American occupation. But it
proved a disappointment to most Japanese because it lacked
a definite doctrine and because its sects were so numerous.
Catholicism, on the other hand, has proved attractive to
teachers, students and educated young people. Preaching
seems to be most successful in districts that suffered most
during the war. Catholic associations for intellectuals are
flourishing: one has a membership of two thousand teachers,
another of five hundred physicians. If, as Mgr Fulton Sheen,
auxiliary bishop of New York, suggested at a conference in
1947, "Asia is to be the battleground of the future between
Christ and Antichrist", what will be Japan's rôle in this
struggle?

Notice particularly the number of converts among women. It has several causes, chief among them being the large number of Catholic schools for girls, closely followed by the importance of our Lady in Catholic devotion and thought.

The Japanese prelates themselves say that if the Church is to be strengthened, it must go out in search of the humble. This will not be easy: their traditions make the people of the countryside and little towns almost impermeable to Christ's message. Conversions are less difficult (although they are always limited to individual cases) among those who have been resettled among the workers in the towns—a class brought into being by the ever-increasing speed of industrialization in this country. If the Church is to accomplish its task, it must lay stress on its nature and its social works, rather than on its magnificence. The Japanese hierarchy has great hopes for Catholic Action, especially Workers' Catholic Action, and increased charitable works: St Vincent de Paul societies and the Legion of Mary are particularly active. They are also looking to young people, for their outlook was radically changed by the events following the last war. Recent signs of a friendly attitude on the part of the government should make it possible for knowledge of the Catholic religion to spread in Japan.

Fr Vallade of the *Missions Étrangères de Paris,* and Miss Reiko Kitahara of Tokyo, two completely different personalities working in the same field, are witnessing to Christ through a work of charity which is having a profound influence throughout the country. Fr Vallade's moving experiences among the very poor living in the Shinkawa district of Kobe have paralleled those of Abbé Pierre. Received at first with suspicion, and indeed some hostility, he began by making friends with the children and then, to be able to help his flock, took Abbé Pierre's advice, and himself became a ragpicker. He managed to buy a piece of land and with the help of volunteer labour built a shed in which to keep his strange collection of belongings; finally, with help from various sources—particularly the French Consulate, which arranged a huge carnival for his benefit—he was enabled to build a permanent house, with a vast warehouse for sorting rags, a little chapel and rooms for ten of the poorest of the poor. The building was ceremonially blessed on December 8th, 1956.

A similar experiment was made at Tokyo by Maria Reiko Kitahara, the daughter of a professor of agronomy at the university. In 1950 she left everything, including her family and her comfortable life, to devote herself to the rag-pickers of Tokyo's "Ant Town". For eight years until her death she devoted herself to these unfortunate people and herself picked rags with them. By her example she saved the rag-pickers' families, for the "Town" seemed certain to be broken up in the carrying out of plans to modernize the capital—and a few days before her death in 1958 she had the pleasure of hearing that the municipality of Tokyo was going to build a new "Town" to rehouse those dependent on her.

Korea, too, has undergone terrible trials. The country was divided as long ago as 1945, and in 1950, when they invaded the South, the northern armies came very close to imposing the Communist yoke on the whole country. Now the agony is over, the country is continually searching for political stability. The two vicariates and the abbey *nullius* of the northern area now form part of the heroic Silent Church. In the part that has remained free, there are 286,000 Catholics in a population of 21,350,000, divided among eight vicariates, four of them entrusted to the native clergy, and the other four to foreigners. In the country there are also 78,000 catechumens and 349 priests (210 of whom are Koreans, almost all seculars); among the foreigners, the strongest group are the Irish (forty-six), followed by the Americans (thirty-four) and the French (twenty-eight). 168 major seminarians are preparing themselves to reinforce the forces already in the field; twenty-six brothers, 819 sisters and 1,652 catechists help the missionaries. Evangelization seems to be going well: in recent years, there have been more than 20,000 baptisms a year, in spite of the presence of numerous Protestant missions, encouraged by the Americans, but divided among themselves. The destruction wrought by war has made the problem of training native priests acute: at the end of 1954 there was not a single seminary left in Seoul. Vocations among women (to the Sisters of St Paul from Chartres, the Carmelites and three local congregations) are restricted by lack of convent buildings. Besides this, the war has led to the overcrowding of the orphanages (at the end of 1954 there were close on 3,000 children in Catholic orphanages, and that figure represents rather less than a tenth of all the children abandoned).

The missions also conduct three high schools: two at Seoul with 189 boys and 305 girls respectively, and one at Taegu with 375 pupils. In addition, they direct nine middle schools for boys with 7,500 pupils, and twelve for girls with 3,800 pupils. The work done by the Korean laity is worthy of note: through their activities the number of baptisms is growing year by year. Between 1957 and the end of 1959, there were almost 100,000—61,000 of them between July 1957 and June 1958. A quarter of them are due to the work of the Legion of Mary. A Catholic university is being built at Seoul.

In the world today, the existence of Formosa is contradictory to logic, yet the island is the most symbolic of bastions against Communist expansion. The island is four times as large as Corsica, and has a topography with mountain peaks of 10,000 feet high, and cliffs along the coast rising vertically 5,500 feet out of the sea. The climate is tropical with abundant rainfall and there are luxuriant forests. Under Japanese occupation (1894–1945) the island was transformed into an industrial and agricultural power of the first class, with about 1,800,000 acres of rice fields, about 5,000,000 acres of forest and about 22,000,000 acres of arable land. There are now about nine million inhabitants, of whom 150,000 are aborigines living on the high plateaux, and two million are Chinese refugees. The number of Catholics increased from 20,000 in 1953 to 115,000 in 1957, with 73,400 catechumens. The archdiocese of Taipeh is the see of Mgr Kuo, a refugee from continental China; one of the four prefectures has also been given to a refugee. Among the 466 priests there are 145 Chinese preaching the Gospel on the island. Unfortunately there are only five major seminarians and it will be several years before a truly native clergy comes into being. A remarkable example has been set by the prefecture of Hwalien founded in 1953 where, two years later, there were already 4,000 baptized Catholics and 17,000 candidates for baptism, distributed among 134 mission stations stretched out over a distance of eighty miles, only thirty-four of the stations having their own chapel. Within the area there is a population of 350,000; 100,000 of them being aborigines. The number of baptized Catholics is today more than 30,000 and there are as many catechumens, almost all of them aborigines. In the district there are sixty-five priests today, as against twenty-one in 1953; the first natives to be ordained are among them. Ursuline nuns from France opened a school in 1958 with the help of Chinese sisters. The hierarchy has just been established on the island and the prefectures will from now on rank as dioceses. The greatest success obtained in the diocese of Hwalien is not so much the fact that so many people have been baptized as that the aborigines, who so recently were head-hunters, given to lechery and drunkenness, have radically changed their habits. The big problem is still that of missionary personnel (in 1960 there were still only forty-three students at minor seminary) for it is said that if there were enough priests there would be at least three million Catholics here (a third of the population) within ten years. Formosa is face to face with Communism: is it going to play in Asia the rôle played in the fifteenth and sixteenth centuries by Hungary against the Turks?

However, not all the Chinese who have left continental China are now living in Formosa. Often because they lack the means, most of the refugees have been unable to get beyond Hong Kong and Macao—and are very happy at having succeeded in finding a haven of liberty, but at the price of terrible poverty. Despite the frighteningly close watch that is kept, not a month passes without the announcement of the arrival of new escapees. Moreover, the Chinese character is such that Chinese are to be found scattered all over the world, in communities ranging in size from a few families to more than a million persons (San Francisco's famous Chinatown has 100,000 of them). Altogether there are more than thirteen million—twelve and a half million of them in Asia. Mgr van Melckebeke has compared their dispersion with the Jewish diaspora. In this great body of people there are 300,000 Catholics—and they too have their priests, 432 of them (322 in the communities scattered throughout Asia according to figures published in 1953). The expulsion of missionaries from China has made it possible to put 400 more priests at their service and, to provide for their spiritual welfare, the Holy See has nominated a vicar apostolic of East and North Asia for the Chinese of the diaspora: he is Mgr van Melckebeke, the exiled bishop of Ningsia, now at the Scheutist mission at Singapore. By organizing an Information Office in conjunction with 118 priests in fifty-two countries, and by publishing three periodicals in Chinese and arranging a correspondence course of instruction in religion, he has started a movement giving exiled Chinese effective spiritual and material help.

CHAPTER V

THE NEW WINE

In recent years the missionary Churches have had to face problems hitherto unknown, although foreseen by the popes, and especially by Pius XI. They spring from the fact that the races of Africa and Asia, so recently under the guardianship of the European nations, have awakened and, becoming aware of their adulthood, have turned their thoughts to claiming their independence and their right to be masters of their own destinies.

The movement began before the last war, but it has become more marked (and very rapidly) since 1945. The first to demand their independence were the countries with an ancient civilization and traditions. But races that had never had a very advanced civilization, and have never been nations in the sense in which we in Europe use the word, have also laid claim to the right of independence within the framework of the administrative boundaries created piecemeal and often completely artificially by the colonial powers. The emergence of new States has not always taken place undramatically: the training of a native élite by the protecting powers, by setting up a secular and often materialist ideal, has thrown these new upper classes off their course, for the natural thing was for them to grow up in a milieu wholly imbued with a very powerful pagan spirituality. The result is that they have become an easy prey for evil shepherds. The fact that international Communism has come to power in some long-civilized countries has aroused a storm that has not yet completely died away. Where Communism has assumed power, Catholics are completely cut off from their brethren in the rest of the world, and are subjected to all kinds of annoyances, and to persecution and diabolical temptations. Where Communism has not as yet penetrated, what will be the lot of Catholics? What form will relations take between the Church and the new leaders? What will be the position of foreign priests? There are so many burning questions. Our next task is to try and glimpse possible answers to this problem in the Afro-Asian context; this book concludes by trying to show exactly what is meant by that pitiful phrase, the Silent Churches.

THE CHURCH AND THE NATIONALIST MOVE-MENTS IN AFRICA AND ASIA

In the last thirty years more than thirty peoples have broken the bonds linking them, sometimes for several centuries, to the colonial powers that had discovered them, and for reasons both of prestige and trade, had imposed on them a guardianship which gradually became humiliating to the leading classes, whether they had been created by the colonial powers or were the offspring of ancient civilizations. After Arabia and Iraq (1932), Egypt (1936), Syria, the Lebanon and Ethiopia (1941), first Asia and then Africa, profiting from Europe's growing weakness, either recovered or laid claim to independence: first Korea, profiting by the defeat of occupying Japan (1945); then Jordan and the Philippines (1946); India, Pakistan (created piecemeal on the sole criterion of Islamic religion) and the Yemen (1947); Ceylon and Israel (another purely religious creation in 1948); Indonesia (1949); Libya (1952); Vietnam, Cambodia and Laos (1954); Tunisia, Morocco and the Sudan (1956); Malaya (1957); Ghana (formerly the British Gold Coast, 1957); Guinea (formerly French Guinea, 1958); and the republics formed from the former French African colonies, British and Italian

Somaliland, Nigeria and the former Belgian Congo (1960). The movement has not yet finished: the old British East African colonies (Kenya, Tanganyika, Uganda, the Rhodesias, and Swaziland) are official candidates for independence. Asia, the more advanced continent and the first to free itself from European tutelage, is continually offering its hand in friendship to Africa and proposing joint action so as to bring into being against the white races (who are divided into two ideologically conflicting blocks) a Third World, capable of putting decisive pressure on the direction of world events. This was the programme of the famous Bandoeng Conference of 1955. Christians have not so far been inactive in this coming together, and they must not be so in the future. Their activities may, indeed, be of primary importance as far as the future is concerned. Anti-Christian forces are not inactive— far from it, and Christians, having within their ranks, especially in Africa, groups of leading citizens remarkable in size and quality, should act as a moderating influence on the new forces of nationalism. For its part, the Church must still further increase its endeavours to preach the Gospel, for Christ's teaching is the answer sought by these young Christian leaders to the problems facing them in their new political adulthood.

While old Asia goes on living more or less within the framework of its traditions, and has always had classes with a high level of intellectual culture, young Africa has awakened suddenly, as a result of its contact with European civilization. It should not be forgotten that in twenty-five years Africa has advanced as it were from Merovingian times to those of the French Revolution. But in Africa, all the intermediary stages still coexist with the jet age. What then is surprising about the fact that there is some disorder and near confusion? The nationalism in question undoubtedly possesses an educated character: just as it was the intellectuals of the middle class who created the French Revolution, so it is the

intellectual élite of Black Africa who are leading the struggle
for independence. Only exceptionally does this intellectual
nationalism present the xenophobic and aggressive character
of Asian nationalism.

What is the Church's reaction to the attitude taken by the
nationalists? When missionaries have been regarded as
"colonialist spies", she has always reacted by proclaiming
with the popes, and especially Pius XII, the supranational
character of the Catholic Church, and by establishing, sometimes even precipitately, a native hierarchy. When necessary,
her missionaries have not hesitated to adopt the nationality
of the country in which they carried on their missionary work
in order, as in Indonesia, to be able to continue to teach the
native clergy who will finally be called on to replace them.
But when a State claims the right to restrict human freedoms,
and to use for its own exclusive benefit all the forces at work
in the country, the Church protests violently, and does not
hesitate to go even as far as martyrdom to oppose totalitarian-
ism. Against an arrogant State she will also defend the rights
of oppressed minorities and the free exercise of political
rights by every citizen. In the Encyclical *Fidei donum* (April
21st, 1957) Pius XII put Catholics on their guard against
false nationalism "stirring up passions, making peoples and
races rise against one another, making use of real difficulties
to seduce minds with easy mirages or to sow rebellion in
hearts".

In all the countries that have recently won their independence, in joint letters local bishops have given reminders of
the teaching of the pope on this subject; they write of the
legitimacy of aspirations towards independence provided that
it does not degenerate into blind nationalism, and of the
necessity of everyone working for the common good after
emancipation, and of the Church's incompetency to declare
in favour of this or that form of emancipation or political

scheme. At Christmas, 1955, the Indian bishops recalled this point in a joint letter:

> The movement for political and social changes which, in one form or another, has affected all the Asian countries in the last half-century is basically an expression of the legitimate aspirations of the peoples of Asia for national independence, political democracy and social reforms. As such it merits the support of the forces of Christianity throughout the world.
>
> In its best form this movement has been a legitimate protest against obsolete colonial imperialism and economic exploitation, and has in a large measure freed the Asian continent from these evil parasites.
>
> At present the movement is itself threatened by a new and deadly enemy: the imperialism of international Communism. Just as the peoples of Asia have protested against the old evils of colonialism, so they should now repudiate the efforts of Marxist communism, which is trying to turn to its own sinister ends the movement towards freedom in Asia. . . .
>
> The new societies which have grown up in Asia are threatened not only by Communist imperialism and the remnants of colonialism, but also by the national antagonisms which have begun to appear between the Asian peoples themselves. If the final outcome of the struggle for national liberty were to be exaggerated nationalism, that would be a betrayal of the aspirations of millions of Asiatics.

If in this extract we replace the words "Asia" and "Asian" with the words "Africa" and "African", it would be just as valid for the black continent. Indeed, it was in identical terms that the bishops of the Cameroons (April 11th, 1955) and those of the countries formerly making up French West Africa and Togoland (April 24th, 1955) expressed this problem. In a declaration dated June 29th, 1956, the bishops of the Congo (then the Belgian Congo) and of Ruanda Urundi emphasized the fact that "it is not for the Church to pronounce on the forms to be taken by the emancipation of a nation. It considers it legitimate from the moment it is accomplished with respect for mutual rights and charity."

Papal solicitude for the young nations has never been more clearly manifested than in the Encyclical *Fidei donum,* already referred to several times. In it Pius XII declares firmly that establishment of a native hierarchy does not point to the end of missionary activity; and that the interest shown by the Church in Africa's political evolution will not prevent her protesting against any false nationalism, inroads of atheistic materialism or the fears aroused by the advance of Islam. What is necessary is that men should work to bring into being a Christian social order in Africa. This can be done only if missionary work is increased, so that all districts may be endowed with a stable local clergy. Unfortunately, many of the missions are still too young to reach this stage, for there is still a shortage of personnel. The older missions need to do still more educational and social work, especially through Catholic Action. Faced with the joint threat of Islam and Protestantism, and with eighty-five million animists still to be saved, the missions need the help of the whole of Christendom. The need for priests and specialists is urgent. Some areas have only forty priests for a million souls, of whom 25,000 are converts; others, fifty for two million people, with 60,000 converts: twenty additional priests in such a mission would make possible a great leap forward. But the ultimate aim of missionary work remains the stable and definitive establishment of the Church through the bringing into being of a sufficiently large body of native clergy. The fulfilment of this programme would calm the fears of native intellectuals. Indeed, it is only by deliberately abandoning the traditional, but nowadays useless, pattern that the African Church—like the Asian—will be able to continue to advance.

The new nations are oppressed by the twin dangers of Islam and Communism. This is especially true of Africa. In

Fidei donum, Pius XII drew the attention of the Christian world to the disturbing advances made by Islam, "a religious concept of life which, although calling strongly upon the deity, nonetheless attracts its followers to a way which is not that of Jesus Christ, the only Saviour of all people". But what makes Islam even more disturbing than its missionary activity is the fact that it leads to a form of political life linked indissolubly with the religion of Allah and that by doing so it brings into being a new kind of nationalism—a nationalism wider than local boundaries and state frontiers, the nationalism of *Umma*, the community of Allah, which in the West is quite improperly called "pan-Islam". When talking to intellectuals, the missionaries of Islam teach a philosophy which is, to however small a degree, secularist, so that Communism when it comes finds all ready for it a field in which its pernicious ideas will germinate rapidly.

In Afro-Asian countries, Communism has the impudence to play the nationalist game. To the new ruling classes of intellectuals and officials it presents the alluring picture of Soviet scientific progress and planning. It also encourages that racialism which is always ready to refuse financial and economic help from the West, from fear of a return of colonialism in disguise; it offers its help "disinterestedly" to the young independent nations. Its work is often made easier by the fact that the new leading classes can discern only one ideology in the West, and that is Marxism, for the West tries to appear secularist and neutral. The result is that Communism succeeds in flooding the nationalist movements. As in Ceylon, it will also collaborate freely with governments in power. But generally it prefers to be patient and wait until the fruit is ripe and ready for plucking most easily, and then keep it to itself; thus it will watch sympathetically the setting up of an authoritarian régime which suppresses the opposition in readiness for its own coming to power. What in ten or fifteen years' time will be the political condition of Guinea,

Ghana or Indonesia? What will be that of the Congo, where all the demons of young nationalist movements, anti-colonialism, racialism and tribal rivalries now confront one another? The further course of events already under way in this country, where more than a third of the population is Catholic, should be a matter of concern to us all.

Finally the clandestine activities of Communists who are continuing to work for their own ends are being carried on freely through the channel of youth work. In 1958 there were in black Africa more than twenty youth associations either affiliated with or sympathetic towards Communism, through which the World Federation of Democratic Youth—whose inspiration is notoriously Communist—could transmit its orders and instructions. Against this weakening influence on young minds there is but a single barrier: a clearly understood Catholicism at work in the social sphere. That is why in the lands it controls Communism has but a single immediate aim: the destruction of the Catholic Church, the only organized, and hence the only dangerous, source of opposition.

THE CHURCHES OF SILENCE

In every age the Church has been familiar with persecution. Even in the twentieth century it has suffered—from the war and Japanese occupation throughout South-east Asia and on some of the Pacific Islands (especially New Guinea); from the civil war in Vietnam, and from some rebellions, such as that in Madagascar in 1947, or Colombia in 1948; from brigandage in Manchuria in 1934–5; but also from general and organized persecution. This occurred first in Russia after the October Revolution, when the Orthodox Church especially suffered, as also the Ukrainian Church (of Byzantine Rite, but in union with Rome). Then, in Mexico, from 1917 onwards there was persecution, but especially from 1926–40 (a period reflected in Graham Greene's novel *The Power and*

the Glory). In Spain, during the civil war, persecution was
systematic and cruel: apart from the laity, 7,300 priests,
thirteen bishops, 283 nuns and 249 seminarians were executed. Persecution raged equally cruelly in Nazi Germany
and the countries she occupied: more than 2,500 Catholic
priests and Protestant pastors died in Dachau alone; in the
Baltic countries after the Russian occupation in 1940, more
than 78 per cent of the Catholic clergy had been liquidated
within eight years; in Eastern Europe after the Communists
had seized power in the various countries, we remember the
famous trials of Cardinals Mindszenty and Stepinac, and the
5,000 priests executed from among the Uniate clergy of the
Carpathian Ukraine, and the 2,000 priests either murdered
or imprisoned in Jugoslavia, and especially in Croatia, apart
from the more obscure people, the laymen, seminarists and
nuns. Today Communism rules more than a thousand million
human beings spread over an area equal to a third of the land
surface of the globe. Among these peoples there are sixty-
three million Catholics—7 per cent of the members of the
Church—living in more than three hundred dioceses, a hundred and sixty of them subject to Propaganda.

In 1956 the situation of the dioceses subject to Propaganda
but living under the Communist yoke was as follows:

Albania, five dioceses, two bishops murdered, two dead in
prison; North Vietnam, ten dioceses, one bishop murdered
and four exiled—and more than 800,000 Catholics living in
exile in the South, Laos and Thailand; North Korea, three dioceses, one bishop murdered, one imprisoned, one deported;
China, 142 dioceses, six bishops murdered, sixteen imprisoned, eighty expelled, a cardinal exiled, 2,700 missionaries
expelled, 200 Chinese priests dead in persecutions; from the
single Trappist monastery of Yan-kiaping, twenty-five dead
and fifty imprisoned. The invasion of South Korea by the
Communists was accompanied by bitter persecution, the
most tragic of the happenings during it being the "death

walk", a horror additional to the "normal" massacres, imprisonings and executions.

But the fact is that to study the working of real organized persecution, we must turn to China, both because of the size of the Chinese Church, and because it is possible to trace the pattern of events there.

The persecution of the Catholic Church in China

In 1949, at the moment when Mao Tse-Tung's troops made themselves masters of the whole country, there were in China 3,200,000 Catholics and 700,000 catechumens in a total population of 620,000,000. The Church comprised 142 districts, with twenty archdioceses, ninety-two dioceses, twenty-nine prefectures and a mission *sui juris*. Thirty-three of them were administered by Chinese prelates: four archdioceses (including Pekin, entrusted to Mgr Tien, who was made a cardinal in 1946); twenty-seven dioceses (including Shanghai, entrusted to Mgr Kiong in October 1949) and two prefectures. There were 5,840 missionary workers, of whom 2,350 were Chinese, sixteen major seminaries with 1,937 students, sixty minor seminaries, with more than 3,500 pupils, three Catholic universities, 189 secondary schools, 2,000 primary schools and 2,250 schools of religious instruction and thirty-two Catholic printing houses. A wholly native congregation had been founded by Fr Lebbe and Mgr Costantini, the first Apostolic Delegate in China: this was the Congregation of the Disciples of the Lord, whose present superior is Mgr Kuo, now the archbishop of Taipeh in Formosa. The congregation now has houses in Formosa, Hong Kong and the Philippines, where it is dedicated to missionary work among the Chinese of the diaspora, but the majority of its priests are still in mainland China. And what remains of all this now? Nothing of the educational work, only four churches open in Pekin, and only twenty priests at work there, although in 1949 there were in the capital 179 Chinese priests and seventy-eight foreigners, in a community of 215,000 Catholics. Out of the 5,840 missionary priests there were in China in 1949, within four years more than 5,500 had either been expelled, or have succeeded in fleeing to free countries. And how many of the rest are still free to move about and work?

When taking power the Communist government did of course proclaim freedom of religion, but very soon foreign missionaries were being accused of spying and plotting; then, in their turn, the Chinese priests were persecuted for "plots of a kind giving support to foreign imperialism". This was not of course the first time the Catholic Church had been accused of following an "anti-national" policy: already in 1926, when Chiang Kai-Shek had just taken power with the help of the Communists he later fought so energetically, the Chinese Church was pilloried; Pius XI, by publishing the Apostolic Letter *Ab ipsis* (June 15th, 1926) made nonsense of criticisms directed falsely against Chinese Catholics; recalling that the Church of Jesus Christ is Catholic by nature, that is, she speaks to all the peoples of the world without exception, the pope stated that missionaries serve the interest of the people of heaven alone, and not those of any earthly nation; and that foreign priests were there only to train native priests, to whom when there were enough of them they would entrust the Church of China. The Church claimed no special privileges for herself, but only the strict application of common law.

Mao Tse-Tung's government tried to avoid making martyrs —it was well known in Pekin that they are "the seed of Christianity"—but it sought, systematically, especially after 1950, to bring the Church into disrepute by using the old stock of nationalism and xenophobia to be found among the Chinese people. Hence came the trials for espionage and "anti-patriotic" plots. The rest of the people had to submit to a complete brain-washing, so that every trace of contamination by Christianity (regarded as anti-intellectual) was removed.

The three Catholic universities of Shanghai, Pekin and Tientsin were "nationalized"; the Communist State seized colleges, schools, hospitals and orphanages directed by Christians. It next undertook the destruction of the Church by corruption from within; indoctrinating students, pupils and orphans, who were made to bring accusations against teachers, priests and nuns, so provoking the authorities to intervene "to re-establish order", and also giving pretext for despoliation, the imprisonment of the "guilty" and the expulsion of "foreign spies". The internuncio himself was expelled, and the Legion of Mary, the soul of the resistance, was subjected to constant annoyance as a subversive political organization, whilst Catholic Action was suppressed. The departure of foreign priests weakened the Church considerably for it deprived half the parishes of pastors. Places of worship were confiscated and used for "other purposes". Finally, an appeal was made to patriotism to build up a "national church". "Patriot councils", with one Chinese priest and three progressive laymen, were set up in each parish. Meanwhile, there was a demonstration of friendliness, to rally the Church: the bishop of Sienhsin was discovered in the act of flight, and was begged to return to his diocese without fear; regular ordinations took place in Hankow (at the beginning of 1954) and Shanghai (at the beginning of 1955). Then the dogma of "triple autonomy" was proclaimed—a dogma favouring the new "Chinese Church": autonomy of government (the prohibition of foreign priests), autonomy of teaching (rupture with the Holy See, the bishop becoming the highest authority) and autonomy of maintenance (prohibition of the receipt of funds from abroad). In the etymological sense of the word, this was in fact the *dissolution* of the Church. But progress seemed too slow and it became necessary to have recourse to genuine persecution to impose the new institution on the faithful. It was especially bitter in Shanghai which, after the death of Mgr Beda Tsang, the Rector of the College of

Zi-ka-wei, had become the centre of resistance under the heroic leadership of the bishop, Mgr Kiong; the "refractory" were imprisoned and Catholics were systematically morally terrorized. The indefatigable prelate himself was arrested on September 26th, 1955, together with thirty Chinese priests and religious and a thousand laymen, 300 of them prominent people. It is unknown whether the bishop is still alive.

The last step, with the proclamation of schism, was taken in April 1958: the vicar general of Nankin—the archbishop, Mgr Paul Yu Pin, had managed to flee—one Li Wei Koang, who had been excommunicated by the pope, proclaimed himself the supreme head of the "Chinese Patriotic Church" and went on illegally to consecrate several accommodating bishops with the blessing of the Communist government: two Franciscans at Hankow (April 13th, 1958), four secular priests at Siensin (formerly Tien-tsin, April 20th, 1958), four at Tsi-Nan (June 1st, 1958), two at Kwai Yang (June 15th, 1958), one at Jehol (June 22nd, 1958) and one at Pao Fing (July 22nd, 1958). These consecrations were of course irregular because they were performed without papal nomination of those consecrated: the "bishops" were named "by the people" (that is to say, by the Communist authorities, who had the effrontery to add "in conformity with the ancient practice of the Catholic Church"). It will be remembered that a similar attempt to set up a schismatic Church was made in Czechoslovakia in 1949–50; it collapsed. The position of the Chinese Church is similar to that of the Church in France under the Revolution: pray God that like its elder brother, it will come triumphant through the trial!

The Chinese schism was a very bitter blow to Pope Pius XII—from which he never recovered. With all his strength he supported the heroic resistance of the faithful, especially in three Encyclicals, *Cupimus imprimis* (January 8th, 1952), *Ad Sinarum gentem* (October 7th, 1954) and *Ad Apostolorum Principis* (June 29th, 1958). He showed his solicitude for the

persecuted in these moving words in the Apostolic Letter
Cupimus imprimis addressed to the "bishops, clergy and
faithful of China":

> Above all we desire to show you our ardent affection for
> the whole Chinese nation. Since the most remote times, China
> has been distinguished among the other nations of Asia by its
> high deeds, by the monuments of its literature and by the
> brilliance of its civilization, and once it had been illuminated
> by the light of the Gospel, which vastly surpasses the wisdom
> of this world, it drew from it the greatest spiritual riches, that
> is the Christian virtues, which perfect and confirm the natural
> virtues. For the Christian religion, as you are aware, does not
> contradict any teaching which is true, or any institution in
> private or public life, provided it is inspired by justice, freedom
> and charity, but rather encourages, sustains and helps them
> grow.

This is why the pope spoke of his sorrow and that of the
Christian world on seeing the attacks to which the Chinese
Church was subjected: to adhere to her, he said, is not to lack
patriotism; but the Catholic Church, being universal, cannot
be made to serve any particular nation, and cannot allow the
formation of a Church separate from Rome: "A Christian
community which acts in such a way will dry up, like a vine
shoot cut off from the stock, and will not be able to produce
the fruits of salvation." He spoke in justification of foreign
missionaries who "indeed seek for nothing more, and long
for nothing more than to adopt your country as a second
fatherland". He exhorted the faithful to remain strong, pray
for their persecutors and invoke the help of the Chinese
martyrs to support them in their trials.

On October 7th, 1954, when the "triple autonomy" had
been demanded of the Chinese Church by the Pekin government, the pope replied with the Encyclical *Ad Sinarum
gentem* in which he said that, despite the heroic resistance of
the Christian community as a whole, some people had yielded

and that it was his duty to refute the allegations of the Communist authorities. Autonomy of government was unimaginable, for even if there were no more foreign priests, the Church would remain united with the Vicar of Christ, for such was our Saviour's own command. Administrative autonomy, even if highly desirable, could not set itself up against the fraternal bond between Christians. Lastly, autonomy in teaching comes up against the hard fact that although preaching should be adapted to the special outlook of each nation, the Gospel cannot be interpreted in more than one way. In conclusion, the pope recalled the supranational character of the Catholic Church and condemned any movement towards a "national church", calling it the negation of the catholicity desired by Jesus Christ for his Church.

The situation having grown worse, in the Encyclical *Ad Apostolorum Principis* (June 20th, 1958) the pope solemnly condemned the "patriotic" societies aspiring to lead Catholics into atheistic materialism, and recalled that it is an act of very grave indiscipline to claim to nominate bishops without the Roman pontiff. Referring to the canons (and in particular, canon 953), he affirmed that "no person, or assembly of priests or lay people, can arrogate to himself the right to nominate bishops; no one can legally confer episcopal consecration without prior certitude of a pontifical mandate".

By this time the step had already been taken, but the world did not know it. Pope John XXIII, at a secret consistory on December 15th, 1958, deplored the unhappy situation in the Church of China, and renewed his exhortations to the faithful to be firm, reminding them of the example of martyrs in previous centuries.

CONCLUSION

If, at the end of this little book, whose only purpose has been to give, within the framework of this series, a glimpse of modern missions, we were compelled to sum up in a few words the situation as it appears in the middle of the year 1960, we could find no clearer way of doing so than by saying that our feelings were those of great joy, intermingled with some measure of unconcealed disquiet.

There is great joy at the prospect of the progress made in the last forty years and of the remarkable advances made by peoples so recently obscure—just as the region of the Roman Empire chosen by God as the place of his birth from the womb of a Virgin was obscure—the peoples of Formosa, Ruanda and Urundi. There is great joy, too, for the leading citizens of the young nations whom the Catholic Religion, by its teaching and its charity, has raised up. We find great joy in contemplating the first fruits of the coming harvest: in 1970, if conversions and baptisms continue at the present rate, the number of Catholics in mission countries will be more than 70 million, and Africa alone will contribute 45 million to the total.

Yet there is disquiet at the prospect of the present lack of missionaries, and of a native clergy of high quality but growing in number at a rate below what is desirable. We feel disquiet, too, at the political evolution of some new nations, for their ethic seems to be far removed from the Christian ideal of brotherhood and charity. And disquiet, too, in the face of the combination of the forces of evil using all their ingenuity to heap up obstacles in the path of the propagation of the religion of Love, seeking to ruin from within what toil and struggle have built up.

It is therefore essential for all Catholics to take their share of the difficulties and responsibilities inevitable in the spreading of the Kingdom of God, not only by giving alms, but by constant prayer, positive action suited to their circumstances and through many vocations, for the harvest gives promise of being fruitful, as long as there are labourers enough. We have, however, seen that they ought to be multiplied tenfold —and even then they would still have more than enough to do. For the final aim of the Church is to bring every human being, without exception, to share in the graces of the Redemption.

SELECT BIBLIOGRAPHY

In this series: DE VAULX, Bernard: *History of the Missions.*

BROWN, W. E.: *The Catholic Church in South Africa,* London, Burns and Oates, and New York, Kenedy, 1960.

BURKE, T. J. B.: *Catholic Missions: Four Great Encyclicals,* New York, Fordham Univ. Press, 1959.

CHAMPAGNE, J. E., O.M.I.: *Manual of Missionary Action,* Ottawa, Éditions de l'Université, 1947.

CONSIDINE, J., M.M.: *Across a World,* New York, Longmans, 1942; *New Horizons in Latin America,* New York, Dodd Mead, 1958.

COUTURIER, C., S.J.: *The Mission of the Church,* London, Longmans, and Baltimore, Helicon, 1959.

DANIÉLOU, J., S.J.: *The Salvation of the Nations,* London and New York, Sheed and Ward, 1949.

FREMANTLE, Anne: *Desert Calling,* London, Hollis and Carter, 1950, and New York, Henry Holt, 1949.

HOFINGER, Johannes, S.J.: *Liturgy and the Missions,* London, Burns and Oates, and New York, Kenedy, 1960.

LATOURETTE, K. S.: *History of the Expansion of Christianity,* 7 vols., London, Eyre and Spottiswoode, and New York, Harper, 1939–45.

LOEW, M. R., O.P.: *Mission to the Poorest,* London and New York, Sheed and Ward, 1951.

MURPHY, E. L., S.J.: *Teach Ye All Nations, The Principles of Catholic Missionary Work,* New York, Benziger, 1958.

OHM, T., O.S.B.: *Asia Looks at Western Christianity,* Edinburgh, Nelson, and New York, Herder, 1959.

SHEPPARD, Lancelot C.: *Charles de Foucauld,* Dublin, Clonmore and Reynolds, 1958.

VOSS, G., S.J.: *Missionary Accommodation, A Study of its History, Theology and Present Need,* New York, Society for the Propagation of the Faith, 1946.

WARD, Maisie: *France Pagan?* London and New York, Sheed and Ward, 1950.

Papal Documents concerning the Missions:
In addition to BURKE, T. J. B., above, see also *The Popes and the Missions,* containing complete English translations of *Maximum illud* (Benedict XV), *Rerum Ecclesiae* (Pius XI), *Evangelii praecones* and *Fidei donum* (Pius XII); also *Schism in China,* Pius XII's *Ad Apostolorum principis,* London, Sword of the Spirit, 1959–60.

The Twentieth Century Encyclopedia of Catholicism

The number of each volume indicates its place in the over-all series and not the order of publication.

PART THREE: THE NATURE OF MAN
29. The Origins of Man
30. Evolution
31. What is Man?
32. What is Life?
33. What is Psychology?
34. Man in His Environment
35. Man and Metaphysics
36. Psychical Phenomena

PART FOUR: THE MEANS OF REDEMPTION
37. Prayer
38. The Nature of Mysticism
39. Spiritual Writers of the Early Church
40. Christian Spirituality of the Middle Ages
41. Post-Reformation Spirituality
42. Spirituality in Modern Times
43. What are Indulgences?
44. Mary The Mother of God
45. The Marian Cult
46. What is a Saint?
47. What is an Angel?

PART FIVE: THE LIFE OF FAITH
48. What is the Church?
49. What is a Sacrament?
50. Christian Initiation
51. Penance and Absolution
52. What is the Eucharist?
53. What is a Priest?
54. Christian Marriage
55. Death and the Christian
56. Christian Morality
57. Christian Social Teaching
58. World Morality
59. Christianity and Money

PART SIX: THE WORD OF GOD
60. What is the Bible?
61. The Promised Land
62. Biblical Archaeology
63. Biblical Criticism
64. God's People in the Bible
65. The Religion of Israel
66. The Prophets
67. How Do We Know Jesus?
68. The Life of Our Lord
69. What is the Good News?
70. St. Paul and His Message

All titles are subject to change.